Flag of Permanent Defeat

Flag of Permanent Defeat

Ouyang Yu

PUNCHER & WATTMANN

First published in 2019

Published by Puncher and Wattmann
PO Box 279
Waratah NSW 2298

http://www.puncherandwattmann.com

ISBN   9781925780154

Cover image: Ouyang Yu design by David Musgrave

Printed by Lightning Source International

NATIONAL
LIBRARY
OF AUSTRALIA

This project has been assisted by the Australian Government through the Australia Council, its arts funding and advisory body.

Australian Government

Australia Council
for the Arts

Contents

From SOUL DIARY: KEY WORDS[1]

i did make love to a chinese character once
i wrote about that experience in a chinese poem
i don't need to translate it for you
it defies translation
the character i fell in love with and made love to is
艶

if this is not clear enough it is 艶
let me explain:
it contains at least two other characters 豊 and 色
'bean' and 'colour' or 'sex'
if you look at it more closely
it contains another three—, 口 and 巴
'one', 'mouth' and '巴' a character that doesn't usually make sense
i don't know what i said in that poem-i'd have to go back and check it
but just by looking at this image on the left of the character you'd see a woman
wearing a crown, her mouth, and her two tits at the bottom
on the right there is sex with which sometimes means desire if combined with
another
word
this loved character goes back thousands of years
until its simplified version, purified by feminists and communists
in艳
i mean艳
let me just tell you this
that the radical on the left side means 'abundant'

(10.41分, 00.11.5)

---

1 This excerpt first published in *LiNQ*, Vol., 31, No. 1, 2004, pp. 72-3.

i woke up this morning with a sudden realisation
that for me australia is a decade of rejection or accepted rejection
and china doubles that
but what if   湮没
i continue in this thankless calling
more years of obscurity
perhaps

(12.05分, 00.11.6)

屄   I've written a long sequence about you   屄
searching for you changing you playing you flicking you etc
the fact is they don't even include you in their dictionaries
despite the fact that every chinese woman has got it
and every or nearly every chinese at some time in their life
has uttered you in B or b
it's your turn now

(14.51分, 00.11.7)

so what's the big deal?
two words, huh?
尸 and 穴
put them together one on top of the other, will you?
just a body and a hole, no big deal?

(19.05分, 00.11.7)

it's now time for commercial break, we'll be right back:
buy poetry bye poetry buy poetry bye poetry buy poetry bye poetry
買詩買詩買詩買詩買詩買詩買詩買詩買詩買詩買詩買詩買詩買詩買
詩買詩買詩買詩
buy詩buy詩buy詩buy詩buy 買poetry買poetry買poetry買poetry買poetry

(20.56分, 00.11.7)

"月moon浴夜的深静"

月moon浴夜的深静
Dripping
Drip
哗哗的flow清幽

Scent馨隐约soon vanishing
Sweetening
Sweet
叶下gather醉影

忽断忽起sudden smooth
Coocooing
Coocoo
Crystal bird可意呀忽隐

月moon夜的深静
Sleeping
Sleep
缓缓波动着broken银[2]

山重水复

repeated mountains
repeated waters

repetitious mountains
repetitious waters

repetitive mountains
repetitive waters

---

2 25/6/1985, Wuhan.

mountains repeating themselves
waters repeating themselves

M M M M M M M M M M M M M M
W W W W W W W W W W W W W W

Note: 山重水复，pronounced, shan chong shui fu, means mountains re wa-
ters peat.[3]

占拿

那是光绪四年
郭嵩焘出使西洋
他称埃及为"挨及"
他把committee叫做"科密底"
他还把London and China一书书名译成
《伦敦安得占拿》
我在厕上看了笑死
这话若用古语理解
再用今文译出，就是：

伦敦如何才能既占且拿？[4]

残山剩水

Broken mountains, remaining waters
残山剩水

Disabled mountains, remnant waters
残山剩水

---

3 Written on 26/10/04, in Melbourne.
4 参见《郭嵩焘日记》（第三卷416页）。长沙：湖南人民出版社，1982年，
written 1/10/07, in Canberra.

Setting mountains, leaving waters
残山剩水

Lingering mountains, going waters
残山剩水

Ruined mountains, leftover waters
残山剩水

Canshan shengshui
残山剩水

Can Shan Sheng Shui
残山剩水

Surviving mountains, surviving waters
残山剩水[5]

瑞典细节5

晚上6点
我们离开si de ge er mo
双层bus爬上又一座高架桥
黑色的河水
无声地流过
一座板着面孔的城市
我想起蘸满mustard的鲑鱼
我想起Lars
和
昨天在斯德哥尔摩遍地的雨[6]

---

5 Written 25/4/14 in Jiangxi.
6 2004, Stockholm.

17

白人

先把坏事干尽
等过了若干代之后
再来正确对待
以
道歉的方式

从而生生不息

White People[7]

First did the wrong thing
Then, after many generations
Doing the right thing
By apo
logizing

Life goes on thus

日

日久生情
日久也生厌

That is life
It is also love[8]

自言自语

这真是当年他说的自言
自语的时代
有无人听都无
所谓
还是想要人听
还是没有人听
放在那儿，由时间录音
封存
走得很远的人
又回到很近

---

7 This poem, first written in Chinese, then self-translated by Ouyang Yu, written 11/12/12.
8 Written on 17/4/14, in Songjiang.

他对自己说：But who gives
a damn?
By now, he's pretty much forgotten
himself, like most of the times
and his paraphenania: a cigarette
burning itself to the end
still burning, still smoking
itself, like a living being
with no eulogies sung
no last poem published in the wake
of its death
格图现身，又有多少人
look the other way
"千万别放上去
免得遭人
恨"9

自

自己是自己唯一的敌人和唯一的朋友
自己唾弃自己也赞美自己
自白 self white
自由散漫野史
自己对极大多数人的极度鄙视构成了自我的完美
自，只有二横的自，一撇插在眉心的刀
自，在众人眼中看过去是反的
就像，就不像
Let self at self10

---

9 Written 1/5/16, Songjiang.
10 Written 13/1/14, Songjiang.

2.28pm

真的到了一切都无所谓的地步了午觉睡到一点十六分时很不想起来
又很想起来醒来时睁眼的那一刹那是粮局门口那个台阶心想就是这
个台阶我要写那么清楚明白的一个台阶就在拉铁手风琴般大门和面
前一条白色大街之间奇怪的是没有人只有记忆在屋顶高的地方盯着
那儿看翻一个身想还是睡吧想睡多久就睡多久一切都不管它了睡到
何时醒就何时醒反正没事反正有事总也做不完最后还是起来了冲了
一杯咖啡看做爱的emoticons尚属原始时代没有什么值得品味的一个
浪费时间的人calling himself a life-liver or a time-waster or even more accu-
rately a waster of time now more intuited as each time gone by is a universe
that never dies existing side by side with the current one in a mind that is a
container of universes where in one of those ones one doesn't see people or
living beings live an entirely different life e.g. never eating or shitting but
one does see them live minus this or that technology that makes an essential
difference thus forming their own unique universe a being who lives 500 or
1000 years is one who has witnessed these universes one following the other
in sequence in terms of time and who is nevertheless able to live or have lived
all of them in a mixture without being able to tell them apart without need to
已经没有爱和恨了只有挺起不断地挺起这时传来cohen dead at 82的新
闻也并不觉得惊奇as he becomes eternal in his own universe time is a mind
thing a mental matter一块石头肉被刻度切割好写到哪儿算哪儿在梦里
做掉人生才是至境[11]

2.46pm

每天都是这样静静的、静静的

想一直等到雨停

水弥漫开去　　　　　　　举着空枝　　　　　　　密叶在下

不打伞的鸟在雨滴中觅食

---

11 11/11/16, Songjiang.

一月，桂花开了，闻起来有淡香，比八月淡五个月

变态的季节　　　　　law戳心[12]

4.50pm

(part of a diary entry)

Writing till now, having done 2100 characters for today till this sentence: 哎，男人啊，一生就是一个金字和一个精字。And yesterday I did a section involving bilingual texts. I'll write till I drop and I'll write till nothing can win anything. I'll write till everything can only be published posthumously.[13]

8.12pm

雨一直不停地下。从下午，下到晚上。现在想起来了，出去吃晚饭，打着伞，和她一起走时，路上经过一片片叶子，有的大得能盛住好几颗雨滴，又大又亮的雨滴，透过雨滴能看见下面更亮的绿，绿得有些灰白。又想起来了，那个学生爱问，他问到原乡为什么和异乡是一样的。俺的回答是：请参阅《原乡》第一期的发刊词。所谓异乡，就是来自motherland，把motherland的m拿掉，剩下的是otherland。Motherland从来都是otherland，一切都是文字，一切都隐含在文字之中。他说很有意思。我又举了一个例子：不思乡。他立刻接嘴说：哦，Not nostalgic。我说：No。这其实很简单，也在文字之中，只需要一个slash，即：No/stalgia。No就在nostalgia中，就像otherland在motherland中一样，像这样：M/otherland。还有很多，后来都能想起，比如一个声音在赤裸地躺下时说：死了。再也活不过来了。于是在记忆的深处，一个人高高地走过来，俯下身，张嘴含住。光线从缝隙中穿过。湖、湖的水，就在勃起的那边。

---

12 5/1/17, Songjiang.
13 18/11/12, Songjiang.

8.14pm

天真的在看吗?
又用云，在擦脸了

夜里还在看
那只是死亡的眼

雨落平阳被犬欺
约炮约到湖里，或湖边

but I suspect that there's a pessimist
at every heart

& I suspect
that's why few, if any, say anything

positive as if one were born a
critic, crying and crying...

雨又勃起，大了起来
跟天一样大，都是直直的

约炮的雨，卧床的雨
睡过头的雨

星星雨上烟头比雨亮[14]

8.21pm

昨晚11.30分睡，中途起来小便，时间约2.30分，这时已经做了一个
梦，很恶的梦，然后又睡着了，醒来时已经是7.36分。拉开门帘，外
面有阳光，又是一个晴天，但不太晴，天上有彩色的、断层的云。

---

14 2/7/16, Songjiang.

早上看Lidia　Vianu从罗马尼亚发来的消息说，他们也要出Wind　in the　　Willows的罗马尼亚文译本了，因为这是一本关于友谊的书，而"Young readers in communist Romania were besieged by the violence of a lying ideology"。这条消息是今天收到的，来自"Contemporary Literature Press, under The University of Bucharest"。以前几乎不看，现在我得把它收藏起来了。

8.22pm

刚散步回来。之前又感到了难以忍受的静。但穿窗而入的蛙音，在遥远的湖水那边起伏，引得人心也跟着起伏，于是脱去了黑色短裤，穿上了黑色灯芯绒长裤，披上那件黑色的条纹棉质衬衣，把门关上就出去了。

湖上有少有的一个渔人在钓鱼。怎么看得见呢？看得见的。哦，有长长的闪亮的浮筒。一节节的，绿的、红的、黄的、蓝的，文明研制出的野蛮。天不算太黑，路是白的，灰白的，总是绕湖而行。

The feet hesitated where two paths diverged. They had no Frost in mind. But they took the usual one for the simple reason---if there were a sayable reason---that they followed where the past was as the thought of the girl returned: born in 86 or 88? The answer was always a no. How could the poles apart come bound together? The feet had no thought of their own; they stepped out, one after another.

林木幽美，但看不见。现在又回到了那条，曾经围满了开花的野油菜花的路。Wild canola早已收割，their corpses躺在路的两边，在黑暗中发白。这地方依然开着花，in the darkness，这些flowers似乎是黄的，但眼睛知道，它们在白天是white，而且间有蓝花。只有夜和独人的眼睛在看。

A man sat on the step reading his mobile phone, his face paled with the illumination, and he was smoking. Somewhere came a plonking sound. A fish that led the eye in search of its trace. All wrinkles of old water.

两条旧船，仍在它们躺了很久很久的地方。船身有很多破洞，长着稀稀拉拉的荒草。这样它们也似乎很满足，[15]

8.30am

自杀成熟了 　　　　一个雨点都能促成 　　　　夏天在下
栅栏镶了亮珠 一张脸

曾是胯下的桶 　　　多就少了 　　　远方不是人 　嘴脸是那些
不愿再见

Goodbye 　　thank you 　　goodbye thank you 　　goodbye 　　no thanks[16]

8.36am

like a creed
that grows up
suddenly over
crowding the skies
like a 花圈[17]

8.40am

Memory对梦是很不客气的
It's not a profitable thing
The meng, I mean, is like the feng
掠过水面不留痕，　after the traces are seen
梦is not the moon although it resembles it
to a large度in sound

---

15 27/5/16, HBL.
16 25/6/16, HBL.
17 3/7/16, HBL.

a head that you have you carry through the 日
only to be captured and felled by the meng at 夜
it's funny, though, that the meng is not the feng
but they are close to each other in 本质
why worry, then, about the moon not being 梦 or 风
as long as you retain the way it traces your 脑
that initially, and, finally, is 空？ [18]

9.39pm

我找到People
找到那个名字
那个配有电子邮件
地址的名字
找到Delete
并按下了Delete
电脑显示说：
You have removed the person from your contact list
是的，我用无声对它说
我没有感到空虚
我反而感到满足
那是一个未亡人
我也是 [19]

10.21am

吃完了。刚才发在微信上的一个剪影：从窗户望出去的一个城市侧面，还带着窗框的照片，引来Mr Left的问话：在哪儿潇洒啊？

我稍微迟疑，回答了：South半球。
现在想想，还可以改为：在South Half Ball。 [20]

---

18 8/11/16, HBL.
19 2/5/13, YSH.
20 12/7/16, Sydney.

10.52pm

我不觉得它是在哭
也不觉得它在笑
这么久了，它一直在叫
一刻不停地叫
我在做别的事，更感到了寂静
所有的聚会，不能让我安宁
but if it is a she
it must have been her persistent calling
for a mate
the silence that is the rest
of the night, listening
for something that refuses
to respond
the deep eyes of the stars
closed once again
它在10.30几分的时候
关上了啼叫的灯[21]

11.01am

一个叫Zoey Winters的人今天发信给我说：

> u are totally beautiful & pretty! I like ur twitter photos so much. I
> wish 2make out with you ASAP. plz sms me & hurry up, here's my
> nmbr +1-678-586-4427 rofl.

跟着我就发现，她还给包括我在内的至少6个人群发了这封信。

无论如何，她第一句话（"你绝对美丽漂亮"）值得放在这儿，因为
这是我一生听到的最好也最不合适的话。只能相信其6分之1。[22]

---

21 25/6/16, HBL.
22 1/8/15, Kingsbury.

12.23pm

刚去邮局，在路上走去走回，寄了一本我的FF（*Fainting with Freedom*）给Paperback Books的Rosy了，但愿她能卖出去。路上阳光灿烂，我喜欢树的影子，有的是一整棵，有的是稀稀疏疏的影子，还有的就那么几枝。我都会停下，看一看或者照一照。放了一张电线杆的影子到微信上，无人理会。想起那个爱发微信的小伙在，每次发一张照片，比如一朵花，还要配上"这是一朵花"，又比如一朵云，要配上"这是一朵云"。是他自己stupid，还是他以为别人都stupid?[23]

50页

在澳大利亚写长篇拿去投稿
出版社无一不给以下面这个警告：

Please submit no more than 50 pages
And we shall read more if we deem it interesting enough

译成中文
便是：

投稿时请勿超过50页
除非足够好看，否则到此为止

记得我投烦了
这么告诉他们：

But my story only begins
At page 51 and it does not become interesting until page 101
译成中文
便是：

---

23 Ditto.

我讲的故事只在
51页开始，且只在101页后才开始好看

结果可想而知，我的长篇
在他们手上，永无出头之日

但是，但是，一旦百退之后发表
又总是不入围就拿奖

至于个中原因
此处按下不表[24]

56 pills

一双美目，就在回头的一刹那
被我盯住
我后来告诉她：You've got such
beautiful eyes！
我们去兰桂坊吃饭
她趁洗手的当儿
撂给我一首英文诗
"59 Pills"
我看了，看不懂
只觉得扑朔
迷离
那餐吃得很贵
大约500来港币
没要她付钱
她付的是故事：

24 6/5/14, YSH.

嫁了一个多伦多的
doctor老公
有钱，没话说
有天吵架，一气之下
当晚飞回香港
从此独身一人
我没把她骗回宾馆
我没这种能力
但我还是特别喜欢
她那双动心的美
目
后来在多年（大约14年）的聊天
的晚上
我又想起了56颗pills
不禁打了一个寒颤：My God！
那是一睡就是亿亿年的
药丸啊
可那双美目
一直埋在我的心
缝[25]

1796-1803

这段时间，中国人干了什么
我不知道
他们照样吃了喝了拉了撒了看了玩了完了走了
什么都没留下
只留下一些让后人纳闷
是否属于Chinese的坛坛罐罐
一个字没有留下
Matthew Flinders没这么干
他开了一条船

---

25 15/10/16．HBL.

吃没吃什么
喝没喝什么
倒是写下了整整
9年的日记
都是字
记下了去过的无数地方
1803年的2月16日
他说，他把一个刚去的地方
命名为：Melville Bay[26]
梅尔维尔海湾
这还不算
他更是一反拉丁语的
Terra Australis Incognita
（未知的南方大陆）
而首次命名澳大利亚为
Australia
说：being more agreeable to the ear[27]
（这样听起来更悦耳）
昨天跟朋友饮酒时，我说：
我在湖边住了这么久
还没有为任何物体命名
现在我就做：

把窗前那湖叫做
昱望湖[28]

---

26 参见Matthew Flinders, *Terra Australis*. Text: Melbourne, 2000, p. 201.
27 参见：http://www.slsa.sa.gov.au/encounter/flinders/namingaust.htm
28 10/5/16, HBL.

A fragment

他说：

我觉得生活
表明上看来
极为无聊
极为丑陋
极为单调
里面想必
埋藏着诗
这样生活
才有意义
因此我便
去发现那
秘密的核心
《人树》一书
由是浮现[29]

诸位需知
这是found poetry
原话在此
自己读去：

"I felt the life was, on the surface, so dreary, ugly, monotonous, there must be a poetry hidden in it to give it a purpose, and so I set out to discover that secret core, and *The Tree of Man* emerged."[30]

懒得多说了
一句都不想
多说[31]

---

29 此为欧阳昱对下一段英文引文的译文，但经过了诗意的断句处理。
30 引自Patrick White: https://en.wikipedia.org/wiki/The_Tree_of_Man
31 26/6/16, HBL.

A Mass of Emotions

哈代写苔丝
有这么一笔
说她二八芳龄
是 "a mass of emotions"
这一笔非常传神
却很难翻译
应了我的一个微论：
越简单，越难译
比如
"老大难"怎么译
又比如
"自由自在"怎么译
英语、哲学、历史毕业的
王博士
我酒桌上的近邻
想了一会后说：
莫不是说她
"五味杂陈"
我没则声
后来，我想起中国话里的
"一团和气"
觉得"一团"
和哈代的"a mass"
还比较接近
但"一团感情"
和"a mass of harmonious airs"
就一样说不过去
此话按下不表
等待译坛高人
我则根据直译原则
以及"at ease"的习语
把"自由自在"译成了
"let self and at self"

至于"老大难问题"
也不是不能直译滴：

Something that is old, big and hard to deal with[32]

Bored

在Age of Boredom
干什么都没有兴趣
当农民你得拼命种地打粮食赚取人民币
当工人你得拼命加班开机器赚取人民币
当解放军你得拼命训练舞刀弄枪赚取人民币
当大学生你得拼命擂功赶考试赚取人民币
看杂志杂志要你多学知识多做事（赚取人民币）
看报纸报纸要你多学政治多关心时事（赚取人民币）
看电影电视电影电视要你学雷锋学海迪道德
高尚做好事（赚取人民币）
懒懒散散无所事事令人bored
狂欢喧闹大喊大叫令人bored
花天酒地载歌载舞令人bored
埋头读书不问世事令人bored
bored! bored! bored! bored!
惟有我不bored
我不受任何政治的束缚
我不向任何偶像学习
我不为没钱而伤心落泪
我不为没名而郁郁不得志
我不追求愚人的理想
我不喜欢众人所喜
我讨厌一切陈规陋习
我向往一切新鲜美丽

---

32 26/12/12, Haikou.

我只希望独行其是
我只希望自我独立[33]

All Greek

希腊话：
垃圾：斯科皮迪亚
你好：迪嘎尼斯
你好：雅萨斯／雅苏
苹果：米罗
对不起：西赫诺米
I am good：嘎拉
谢谢：埃夫卡里希多
请：巴勒卡多
Please: 巴拉嘎罗[34]

a more

你需要i
情
你又，得no到
age的mountain
比ocean还g
ao
as cuddly as s
pikes
此时，it's r
ai
ning
kisses, curses, 坑s
伸出去的hands
离horizon

---

33 Written on 27/4/1983 in Wuhan.
34 19/5/15, SUIBE.

只差one mi
ll
i
米
yu宙is an
other
wave费的par
elle
l[35]

Arrival of Winter

最后一片树叶早已摇落
the wind is still shaking the bare branches for what is not there
我在看一些手做的书, listlessly, exhausted even before the arrival
or perhaps because of it眼皮上长了一个小疱
will poetry allow it into poetry? Some misfits, some fuckwits won't
还在等，也无所谓，管它则甚？
The rain is raining in the phone now
很适合自杀的一天，对某个想法来说
Living is so easily hard. Look at an unlit ciggy, the way it waits
忘掉那个人，忘掉那些人，忘掉那些moments
a memory is but a container of wind, winds
终于有活人从C城发来圣诞greetings. Not family
a city of smog, nose-happy smog, and the sound of trees in the风wind
a wind风with a message that goes:

can we go to the canteen for dinner?
if possible at all, can you order me
a re gan mian as i never seem to get it
being always late, even at 5pm sharp?

Followed by another one that goes,

35 19/10/16, HBL.

but if they run out of the broad-bladed noodles
that's fine because the thin-stringed ones are no good
for the hot and dry noodles

盲碌一生，一无所得，得过都不能且过
切，是且，不是具[36]

At self, let self

After he said no to the Nobel Prize in Literature
In his imagination
He was able to turn

The expression 自由自在
Into proper Eng
Lish

He began with a direct
Translation: Self-let
Self-at

Before he settled for
At self, let self
And, finally, to demystify the so-called China

Experts: he played
With 'At 自
And let 自'[37]

---

36 21/12/16, HBL.
37 28/10/12, YSH.

澳不利亚

陈弘沉底一天之后
来电说
他觉得《澳小利亚》
"不错，真有意思"
并让猴子也来一首
就叫《澳不利亚》
对这个命题作文
我拍手称快
说："猴子不写
我写了"
喏，此时，我就在写
澳大利亚的不
就在于它
基本上对一切都说不
你想发表
它reject你
你想要它
为19世纪华人的head tax道歉
它摇头
你想要它
对中国移民放宽尺度
它说no
你想当它总理
它even more坚拒
你看它地图
像不像个No
或者像个Bu
不？
我听见你说了
那就更"澳不利亚"了
总而言之，统而言之，总统而言之
别的没学会
我学会了

"澳小不利亚"
写了一些
亚不利澳的小诗
不是出气，而是出戏
如此而已，而已如此
一言既出
诗马难追
澳不利亚当然好啦
它不，故它在

各位注意，credit goes
To the first two Chinese
Characters[38]

爱

那时，我不缺爱
那人从加拿大写信给我
总会说：I love you
后来他给我来电话
是call collect
害得我跑到市内
那家邮局
的小电话亭里
在约定的时间
准时接他电话
他一说"I love you"
我就笑，觉得太好玩了
他却认真得什么似的
我当时最关心的
不是爱
而是他打那么长时间电话

---

38 11/1/13, YSH.

是不是会要很多钱
后来这爱变
成了恨
他就再也不写信了
只是，我把那件事写进了一个中篇
叫《岛》[39]

Back then

手把书 拿出来，说：你看，是这个样子的。一看，是红的，有竖线，没
竖线，不大记得清楚 　　　　　外面有个包装 　　　　　是盒子
　　　　很多人 　　　　汹涌来去
it's not like that 　　　　　it's something else 你看，声音说 看
了 　　　一个男孩
本该有dick的地方 dick地方 　　很好的alliteration 只有一个白扣子
战俘切入 暂付阙如 有个细节 细到记而不忘的地步
　　　　dick地步 　　　another alliteration 　which is also a third alliteration
I'm about to go to stool
Fuck the dream
if记忆doesn't hold, it means it's nothing worth记得[40]

BB

谈到细节在
小说中的运用
教授便开始
谈他的看书经历
但他还没开口
就自己把自己删去
因为奈保尔那个细节
学生肯定吃不住
他在 *A Bend in the River* 中

39 3/10/15, HBL.
40 27/11/16, HBL.

曾写过一个男子
跟心仪的女子做爱
把B撑开却没有
把自己东西塞进去
而是冲着那B
吐了一口唾沫
恨犹如此，B何以堪
这细节一看就记住
却无法跟人说起
还有一个细节
是哈代《无名的裘德》
里面的那个Arabella
企图诱奸Jude
为了吸引他注意
竟把刚割掉的猪鸡巴
扔到裘德身上去
过后诱他进屋
说她在用乳房孵蛋
想看不？想看不？
Jude看了，后果就是那本书
教授面对学生
这些都难以出口
只好说了一件
自己亲历的事，多年前
他还是童身
听一个已非童身的朋友
谈他的初吻经历
以为定像名著所述
伟大、纯洁而浪漫
结果惊出望外
朋友就那么一句：

她张口吻我
我心想：口怎么这么臭啊！

就是这么个细节
四十三年没齿不忘
说完环顾四周
发现座中一张小白脸
面露喜色，目已散光
仿佛早进入角色
他便直奔主题，问那小白脸：

"口臭"英文怎么说？

小白脸支吾半日
勉强憋出了一句：She smelt bad

No, no, 教授说
英文里说"口臭"
不是说她mouth stinks
而说她有"bad breath"
你滴明白？
简单记之，就俩BB[41]

Biao

Biao，音同标、彪、飙或飚
但我四十年前下放的那个村庄
和我六十年前出生的那个小镇
是这个Biao，而不是那四个Biao
汉字里没有，嘴上却动辄就说
特别是老二到最后忍不住的时候
就会发生的那个动作
我那地方的人就会用这个Biao字形容
比上述所有四个Biao都Biao
这是后话，且说Gu Ting那晚

讲了一个当年，旅行结婚的故事
说是某甲和某乙
一起旅行着去结婚
长途车轮跋涉，到处是眼睛
晚上熬不住，男的让女骑
好在
普遍都睡着，无眼偷窥瞧
鏖战到极处，男的忍不住
一把掀翻女，东西Biao出去
把对面熟睡的那书生
Biao了满眼镜
他伸手一摸便大叫：
谁这么不文明
到处摔鼻涕！
故事讲到此，还是很遗憾
毕竟没有字，能让Biao字现形
不如干脆英文拉倒：
Shoot、shoot、shoot
效果跟Biao一样[42]

一写完，便发给Gu Ting了，但把最后三行改成：

Shoot、shoot、shoot
效果跟Biao比
都是一样滴

Blow

女人安排男人杀死
老公之前
据说给男人发了
两千多条短信

_____

42 7/11/16, HBL.

英文叫sexted
中文虽无类似说法
不妨叫做"短性"
其中一条说：
You drive, and I'll blow you all the way
译成中文便是：
你来开车，我一路吹你
另一条说：
I need your flesh inside me, baby
再译成中文，便是：
我需要你的肉在我里面，宝贝
其他还需要说什么呢？
老公那次没死成
女的被判9年徒刑
那个男的，名字一看就是
希腊人[43]

Boo

我对希望boo抱任何希望
我对理想boo抱任何理想

我boo喜欢被喜欢
我boo赞任何被赞

我boo入流
也boo想入流

我boo杀人
也boo想杀己

---

[43] 本诗所用材料，均来自这篇英文报道：http://www.smh.com.au/national/a-plot-to-kill-20140728-3coa6.html, written 26/8/14, Kingsbury.

我boo爱
也boo boo爱

我boo在
故我在[44]

ing

夜is香ing桂
桂is风ing叶
叶are绿ing水
水is白ing夜

我am我ing你
你are你ing月
月is人ing石
石are云ing夜[45]

不可译

舅舅说
中国成语，之所以
那么难译
是因为它们
出生在
中国这片
难译的土地
比如
好话说尽
或
坏事做绝

---

44 31/3/16, HBL.
45 20/9/1982.

又比如
挖空心思，坐吃山空
还比如
白痴、白话、白干
换了别人
也就点头称是
但偏偏听者有♥
碰上了我这个喜欢硬
译的人
就硬着译了：

No end of good words said matched with no end of bad things done
这是：好话说尽，坏事做绝

Digging for ideas till one's heart and mind run dry
这是：挖空心思

Sitting idle and eating till a mountain becomes hollow and empty
这是：坐吃山空

White idiots, white speech and white doing or white fucking
这是：白痴、白话、白干

我没法跟舅舅这么说
因为我知道，他英语还没好到

称赞我的地步
只好以不诗的方式入诗[46]

---

46 21/5/14, YSH.

不象

这个晚上不象任何晚上
不象早上不象中午不象下午也不象现在9.59分的晚上
不象night不象evening不象昨天晚上
也不象前天晚上也不象2011年12月7号我现在已不记得的晚上
不象wanshang不是象no象not象不elephant

诗歌
能不能不象[47]

别国

二十多年前
他不开心时
爱发怨气
澳大利亚人会用英语
对他说：No one asked you to come
If you are not happy
You can go back where you come from
（没人请你来
你不开心
哪里来，你就回哪里去）
昨天，在松江一个地方
他亲见一个类似的案例
一女抱怨说
中国什么地方的服务都不好
那营业员来了一句：
那你可以到别国
去住
接下来的话，他没记住
我更没记住

---

47 7/12/12, YSH.

他只是心想：这个国家也硬了
硬起来了哈
我无话可说
诗，暂时就写到这里[48]

北京

在北京想念北京
在北京粗大的六月中旬的阳光中
我想起一些人
从碗里出来
我想起一些无仇无怨的无亲
有个人的眼睛歪了
有个人的头发斜了
有个人，又把自己，微信成微信了
无欲的季节
下体冷得可以
穿透的想法，还挂在那年的海边
有吗、有嘛、有哇
it's time to get angry again
or else it'll be too late
their pockets will pocket everything
they design
for themselves
not just to keep a name
alive
but to keep the name
fattened
it's been like that till 6102
they're never fed up with it
never fed up with themselves
while the rest of the world don't give a shit

---

48 23/12/15, HBL.

to get angry with literary excrement
is to waste your life
getting angry with shit
better spend time creating another world
another universe
这些人的资源，大到可以
把自己淹屎[49]

必须

我必须是没有读者的
我才能够写得好
我才能够讲出真话

我必须是在写作时
自认为已经死了
我才能够惊世骇俗

我必须go against the grain
哪怕到go against the brain的地步
一直写到，无法发表

我才能够
写出，自己想看到
而不是别人想看到，的东西[50]

C

Nagambie
厚朴
黑尔普
Shepparton

---

49 19/6/16, Beijing.
50 2/8/15, Kingsbury.

革命的晚节
Wunghnu
钱吉
Tocumwal
Yarrawonga
Berrigan
Jerilderri
Oversize
有些诗是为眼睛写的
有些是为喉咙

你有病to write

风云人物to write

单身的树

桃子尖

Smoon

包养[51]

Close

诗人想以这种方式
结束今天写的诗

那是那天吃鱼
诗人跟Mr He讲的事

他说澳洲那个国家
做编辑的都是女滴

---

51 21/1/16, on my way to NSW.

有一个特别不喜欢他的诗
每次退稿不说

还附言说：这次你非常close
意即差一点点就选用你

什么g8东西！
再也不投稿去

另一个也是
很挑剔的主

但每年总有首把诗
会在她手下发稿

不过她从来退稿
都不加一字评语

有意思的是最近
她退了3首

他写的
"抽象诗"

破天荒地老地破例
来了一句评语：

These are weird
Poems

意即"这些诗
太怪异"

更有意思的事
还在后头哩

前面那个总说
"You are close" 的那个

居然也把他两首
选进要出的诗集

原来那本书
是多人主编的

这下女胳膊
扭不过男大腿了

否则又要来一个
You are so close

今天他至少
写了十首诗

看看天色不早
就此close[52]

出中国记

那时我们出去
是一种灵魂
出窍的出

出外、除外
一减一得二
一加一得四

---

52 29/12/15, HBL.

后来我们再出
就不想再回去
我们? Who are we?

China是瓷
砸碎了再拼接
拼接了再smash

残，兵败将的泥足
继续在生育
出了、出了、又出了

千诗万缕，小楼昨夜
又西风，古道东风
thin horse，粉成了粉的粉丝

诗狂grass
发甩墨滴
挥毫而降脂

女人是别人的
G8属于self
射而夫、泻而夫

城市做了霾馅子
Highheels的欲望
待写、待泻、代谢[53]

---

53 12/6/16, Fuzhou, Jiangxi.

Baby Hill

She is typing up a Chinese poem I wrote in Spain
In which an expression appears called *tongshan*
She thought it is congshan or mountains or mountain after mountain
Till I say to her it is tongshan or a baby hill
Not that the hill or the mountain is young
But that it has a top like that of a new-born baby
Bare of anything, trees grass and least of all, hair

Thus ended her hours of typesetting my Chinese poems
Written across Europe

成语

某人想跟某人好上
physically好上
本来都有情
但也可能均无意
于是某人metaphorically驾鹤
西去，突然
disappeared
那可能无意者急了
很想他、想回来找他
于是就有声音说：
你这叫欲擒
故纵

成语，汉语的一种
无需在死中求死的理论
像法国理论那样
有多少人掉进福柯
和德里达的陷阱

而不自知
也属于metaphorical的驾鹤西去
有了成语
人人都能把
某种情境，对上号了

真的这样吗，某人说
我看不如
把开篇那种情境
称为yu擒
故纵[54]

查

我查Remy de Gourmont时
查到了另一个人
叫Blaise Cendrars
是个在瑞士出生
后来跑到法国混的人
读到一个地方
我看到：As a short story in Paris
he travelled to New York...[55]
猛然意识到，我又读错了
不过，将错就错译出来也不错：

作为一个短篇小说在巴黎
他旅行去了纽约......

写到这里，我不想多写了
以后再找他的东西看吧[56]

54 23/10/16, HBL.
55 原文见此：https://en.wikipedia.org/wiki/Blaise_Cendrars
56 21/7/15, Kingsbury.

葱

把诗一样贱的葱根
葱一样贱的诗
插入小区
偷来的一小
塑料袋的土坷垃
中
hoping that I never will have to chase
after something so cheap, so neglected
and so essential to make a soup
more delicious than other
wise — these bunches
of half
wilted spring
onion
given by the man
and the girl
for free
那男的连看都不看我一下
嘴里嗫嚅着什么
当我问他多少钱时
旁边一个买菜的人说:
送给你了!
就像那些见人就送诗
的诗
人
但我比诗
更需要
葱[57]

---

57 24/5/14, YSH.

D

For deng
For dawn
For done
For dung
For desperate
For dog
For deedeedada
For daisy
For dune
For dong
For day break
For da
For dang
For despair
For dug
For dray
For deep
For denmark
For demon
For doom
For denggao
For dui
For dian
For dot
For date
For dieu
For dengdengdengdeng[58]

---

58 23/5/14, YSH.

Dao

Dao is way or the way
When they say dao ke dao fei chang dao
It can mean a lot of things, such as way can way not ordinary way
Or way can way extraordinary way

Confucius talks about the dao or the way all the time
He says: the dao or the way is not far from people
Or if the way you build is far from people
It is not the way, or the dao

Dao consists of two radicals, a walk and a head
The head above the walk: someone walking, on the dao, or the way
Dao goes with dao li or way reason
Or it goes with dao de or way morality

Dao also is say and when you say something you dao
Dao is what they sang in a song, in the Cultural Revolution
The dao-gainers have much help while the dao-losers
The Americans, have little help

A woman's vagina is a yin-dao or the yin way
Although a man's is not a yang-dao; it is a yang tool rather
A monk is literally a dao-shi or dao gentleman
Where the monastery is where he cultivates his dao, or the way

Daoism or Taoism is nothing but dao-jia or dao family or way family
Not the family way, not in it
Dao recalls the street nearby
Called The Fairway, or, if you like, the Fairdao[59]

---

59 29/2/12, YSH.

De

已经有点小冷了
她走后，更
有点冷

天黑de好快
对面de光破
窗而出

什么都不在夜下
打叉、打叉、打叉
笔笔勾销去

Body parts
除了penis
重新收集整理

要de
要de
Hero无路可走[60]

2, 3

打二，出现"而"
打二三，删去三
留二

脑中出现二三其德
好，英语无法动词的地方
我来动词：to two and three the morality

---

60 13/11/14, YSH.

Fish

魚、、、、、、
、、、、、、
、、、、、、

感觉

天从头上压下来
夜从心里长出去

If this one were not alive
It would not make much difference

骨感诗人
要诗不活命哲学

You would have to lead a philosopher's life
One who would prefer unmarried for good, and for bad, too

诗沉大海子弟兵
痛改前非诚勿扰

Do you think the hollow of the hand is not the heart
Of hand but what word else would move you, a closed mind?

Body-connected writing: an experiment

This is life and death, one inside the other, life into 死, death sucked into 生
The hermaneutics of love making, the philosophy of bodies, two in one
She telling the story, he recording it, his fingers, transported, busy transporting
His eleventh finger, current, concurrently holding her up
Her utterances his semiotics their metanarrative of 生 and 死
It's a movement in spite of itself

An enormous weight fallen on a pen
A desire nailed through
A body having a sit-in inside the tiny house of another body
While writing goes on, orally and digitally
In their cyberspace of love writing this self
Reflexivity in couplets

eng

有一个词叫藏锋
a hidden blade

有一个词叫少言
few words

有一个词叫不露
keeping it concealed

有一个词叫旁观
watching with averted eyes

有一个词叫索居
living the solitude

有一个词叫不屑
beneath one's dignity

有一个词叫慎独
carefully alone

有一个词叫拉绿
spring coming

有一个词叫归真
returning to the true[61]

耳

In *Billy Sing*
A reference is made
To ear-wind

The kind that blows
Past one's ears
Without him hearing anything

And in *Dream Catcher*
A reference is made
To 'ears-akimbo'[62]

Know what that reminds me of?
招风耳
Ears that invite wind

As they are shaped
Like spread fans
Akimbo

Wind-inviting ears
Ear-wind
And ears-akimbo

---

61 1/11/16, HBL.
62 Qtd in Margaret A. Salinger, *Dream Catcher: a Memoir*. Scribner, 2001, p. 315.

Aren't they better
Than some poems
No one wants to ear?[63]

fenfang

yes, he said through a heavy fog
i made it, i did it
i chose his, I chose hers
i called the title 'fenfang'
as you suggested, hehehehe
and david loved it
no, i meant john

我醒来，意识到是他
no，根本就没意识到不是他
似乎想起，原来有这么回事
他在编一个anthology
跟david，不，跟john合编
当时给他，提了个建议
说chinese也有alliteration的
于是说起了"芬芳"
他问什么意思，我便告诉他：
fragrance

这条梦，太贵了
它的出现
踏平了其他所有的meng[64]

---

63 12/19/16, HBL.
64 24/11/16, HBL.

Fly机

这些密密
这些麻麻
这些麇集
这些蝇拥
这些、这些、这些墨渍

这些疑团
这些凝血
这些胶质
这些fly行物
这些、这些、这些欲死

这些弹着点
这些出生入
这些微拟像
这些大祸临
这些、这些、这些拉黑

这些brains垂体
这些half音符
这些poison蘑菇
这些殊death搏
这些、这些、这些菲thin的命[65]

Freedom

是的，就是这个自由
不仅仅是to do的自由
更是from的自由
From prizes的自由

65 14/12/14, YSH.

From praise的自由
From任何人为制造犹如锁链的荣誉的自由
From粉丝的自由
From关注的自由
From"最"的自由
直到from freedom本身的自由[66]

发音

教英语这些年
一些字普遍被发错
比如，product重音在前
却老是被学生发成
proDuct
作为名词的produce
也是如此，本来重音在前
却仍发成重音在后
成了：proDuce
这都是旧话，不去提它
却说昨天
上研究生的翻译课
居然也频频把音发错
一女生把澳洲悍妇Germaine Greer
的名字Germain（杰梅茵）
发成了Germany（杰曼尼）［德国］
一女生把madrigal（牧歌）
发成了：mad rigal
变成了"疯rigal"
更有一女念诗，把
"Loveliest of trees, the cherry now"一首中
的"bloom"一字
念得跟"blood"一样——

---

66 31/12/12, YSH.

64

你懂你就知道
你不懂，我就没法跟你
细说
说了也没意义
那就到此，为止，吧[67]

废人

低着头，永远也不想抬起来的感觉，看着下面地板上的木纹，木纹
像沙纹，在炉红下映着，低头，要是能一直低到胯间、胯下就好，
废人，看着不是废人的那些人在什么玩意儿上列举的一清单什么发
表的字就想笑，木纹，废人眼皮底下看着的木纹，还有那个女的，
用着什么很矫情的一个名字，还是用笔做成的，故称笔名，死后
一定只记得笔名了，feiren，很不生活的一个，不想生活的一个，a
wasteperson recycle station. But they want to purchase that cloud, 把它做
成一个鱼鲊. A yawn. An ejaculatory ai。Which is death. Which is a stain.
Which is waiting, to be washed.那里面的东西，要多可恶有多可恶。The
heads alive with eatables. Stony heads.[68]

风、俗

风，好俗呀
Wind, vulgar[69]

风趣

风interest
wind interest

Or breeze interest
Or gale interest

---

67 17/11/15, HBL.
68 8/1/17, HBL.
69 15/7/15, Kingsbury.

Or stormwind interest
Or cyclone interest

Or tempest interest
Or zephyr interest

Or funny interest
No, yes

Fun interest
Yes, that's right

风趣
fun趣[70]

Letters and characters: 4 for a start

影flunence   shadow

英glish   heroic

A美rica   beautiful

Leba嫩   tender

R, R, R

A word is a translation
        of itself
into many other

---

70 17/1/13, YSH.

```
          words
in the case of
rude or rough or raw
for example
depending on
the text or the con
text. Take get
          as when it becomes get
at or get into
          or get off or
get down
any word is a translation of it
          self in any combination
of circumstances
          till it disappears
into another
          language like粗
or糙or生
          r, r, r
```

Gangnam Style

那年去韩国
我发现了一个不是秘密的秘密

这个国家最原来是不是叫汉国
我不知道

但我知道
这个国家600多年前的史书

都是用汉字
写成

而且这个国家所有的江
都叫gang

汉江叫han gang
江原道叫gang yuan dao

亦即Gangwon—Do
发音类似钢豌豆

江边叫gang bian
江南叫gang nan

这不，刚才在一家电器店
跟一个生客一起

又看了一次gang南表演
PSY钻到一女肛门下

PSY又往一女肛门爬
PSY还模拟了数个挺胯出胯的动作

不由我诗意顿生
何不叫他肛男style

大陆这么喜欢这个肛男
何不哈韩到

把地名改成新版韩名：
肛西

肛苏
肛阴

浙肛
镇肛

长肛
嘉陵肛

大肛东去
浪淘尽千古风流人物

最后来它一个
苍天无语

肛山如画
一片残阳西挂

何如
何如[71]

Gracas[72]

他杀
了41人

都是"for the fun of it"
"为了好玩"

这是他亲
口说的

其中大多数都是女
的

71 2/1/13, YSH.
72 详情请见关于该犯的报道：http://www.smh.com.au/world/brazilian-man-sailson-jose-das-gracas-admits-killing-41-people-for-fun-20141211-125i7c.html

还包括一个两岁婴
儿，因为杀

的时候叫得太
响

他26
17岁杀了第1个

之后越杀越
"enjoyed it"（欢喜）

每杀之前必先调
研

杀过之后
还会想

那个被杀者
"two to three months"

如果不杀
他会感到"uptight"

那是焦虑
不安的意思

据他说，他一点也不
"remorse"（后悔）

除非把牢底坐穿
如果只判一二十年

出来他还会再开杀
戒一

且慢，我们的时代
几乎人人心里
都活着一个
Gracas[73]

Grandfathers、Longing、Sleepless

学期要结束了
Yu教授感到
同学们写英文时
对时间的意识
依然在中学时代
踏步
人在went和was这样的过去时里
依然会突然冒出
I see和I go和we eat
这种
前后时间不符的情况
一说都明白
一下笔，又都不约而同
地糊涂了
为此，Yu教授想
利用最后的时间
让他们做冲刺
无非是多动笔、多写
而已
他找了三个话题
让他们各自选去
想写祖父、外祖父的
可写grandfathers这个话题
想写内心渴望的
可写longing这个话题

---

73 12/12/14, YSH.

想写睡不着觉的
可写sleepless这个话题
结果巡视一圈看下来
写grandfathers的不多
大多都写sleepless
和longing
课堂结束时，Yu教授做了一个结论
说：我发现一个有趣的事实
女性大多都选
"睡不着觉"（sleepless）这个话题
而男性，大家猜猜是什么？
（大家猜不出）然后Yu说：
选的都是"渴望"（longing）
（众男女笑）
一位男生开篇就说：
I'm longing to have a baby boy
（我渴望生个男婴）
至于女生为何sleepless
恕我不公开秘密[74]

工作

来到一个地方
叫Howe Crescent
沿途都是新月
这边不同，那边也不通
在Cameron Road的
第一个Roundabout
拐错了弯
拐回到Grimshaw Road
去了
在Leonard Road又跑错

---

74 17/12/15, HBL.

跑到Cole Crescent
和Champion Crescent的交界处
而把我引进这一切的
是一条叫Judith的路
此刻，我把车
停在Howe Street上
路口的风光无人欣赏
早晨的斜阳乜斜着眼睛
水漫一样漫过
空旷的草地
黑的瓦，白的墙，更白的周围
使得我很想照相
但倒在我车前的树影
更让我留意
几十幢房，无一个人
风，在叶间蠢动[75]

故事

一上来他就告诉我
媳妇跑了。如果不是因为我透露
我是originally from China，他也许可能不会
mentioned it。他说：她is a Singaporean girl
married to my 'middle boy'。我坐着他开的出租
一路从机场，奔往悉尼的CBD
我的818-820刚落地，他就准确地说出：George
Street。我说：Yes
故事结束的时候，我已抵达那座曾经
爱得死去的地方
（请勿加"活来"这个成腐的陈语）
明白了不仅his wife is Thai，而且his son
is also a 'Thai', a step one

---

75 30/7/14, Kingsbury.

他泰国太太对此事的态度很简单：
If she's gone she's gone
Let her go without a word
One day, two things will find you out:
Your sins or your virtues
我和他握握手，我都不知道他叫什么
他也不知道我叫什么
大家都不好意思问
（请你把这翻译成英文
肯定时态不对，用词不准）
但我知道，他是白人
这个城市还在开出租的极少
几个白人
when everyone else is an Indian
A Pakistani, a Lebanese or a Chinese
这个白人的孩子
却被一个Singaporean女的
耍了一顿而不知去向
I've got nothing more to tell you, Mate
Read this poem, work it out for yourself
and forget it[76]

Reading celan the chinese way

Reading celan
I recognized a Chinese in "Lichtzwang"
A light Wang
Just as I did when I listened to a currawong
A bitter Wong

---

76 No date, Sydney.

Hegel

是哪个该死的家伙
把Hegel译成黑
格尔
Marx是马克思
可以思考的
Engels是恩格斯

有恩情的
Heidegger是海德格
那是大海，那是美德

只有Hegel啊
这个白人哲学家
却被无端抹黑

今夜
就让我把你抹白
叫你：白格尔吧[77]

Hi, there

墨尔本冬天的眼珠
灰溜溜地滴着
阳光碎细的色彩
街道袒露着
阴冷
一张女人的老脸说：you look cold
And我的嘴回应：Am I?
阴森森的灰
溜溜的
光照着光秃

---

[77] 4/5/13, YSH.

天在哭
地冷
爆
了 [78]

Himmelfarb

It was the word 'ugly' that caught you
R attention
A word that took you back to that
Long, steep class
Room; you found this
Description that goes:

我谁都不爱
连我自己在内
我倒是有个女朋友
她长得奇丑

A work
Of fiction
Exists outside
Time, waiting, always waiting
Like nothing
Else
Oh, yes, like the colours
Of the sky

I don't love anyone
Including myself
I do, though, have a girlfriend
Extremely ugly

---

78 17/7/15, Kingsbury.

A Jew, not destroyed in German

Y, but dies in si

Lence in A

Ustralia at the hands of B

Lue

Ugly, of course, is the

Word[79]

Hold

我快hold不住了，二八自行车也能这么玩
别吸了，hold不住了
北京也hold不住了，郊区多楼盘降价超10%
终于hold不住了，微软发布iPad版Office
让小情侣们hold不住的三大激情性交姿势
大象做爱全过程，美女hold不住
盘点各国让人hold不住的房事趣闻
这样的无性婚姻，让我好辛苦，坚持了这么久，我再HOLD不住了
牛郎Hold不住了，是的就在昨晚
最有料的河南美食：口水快hold不住啦！
鱼油Hold不住的概念
和男朋友做爱，时间太长，hold不住啊有木有，求支招
反垄断一案中国联通与电信hold不住了
并晒出两张撒娇自拍,令无数深夜难以入眠的网友大喊："hold不住!"
拉开抽屉满眼是钱HOLD不住
职场囧事：招聘遇神人，面试官也hold不住了
野性女性的特质让男人hold不住的魅力
很多MM都开始烦恼起来了，hold不住食欲体重
两个美女激情强悍，男人hold不住了
成熟的味道 hold不住了
坑爹呢，快递也玩穿越？我hold不住了！

---

79 17/5/14, Datong.

重口味食材，你hold住了吗
在英语强力抽送下，汉语，你hold得住吗？

The change of a word

encouraging

engouraging

engooraging

en鼓raging

Tong

Tong is *henyouyisi*
Tong is通is through
Tong would be tongue but for the ue
Tong is痛 is pain

The world has many tongues but little Tong
The world has many ears but little Tong
The world has many words but a lot of Tong or T痛ong
The world has many roads that are ideologically not Tong

Tong is very physical
Tong is tough
Tong is hard to reach at a heart or mind level
Tong, made impossible at the Creation

合璧

half心half意
现实shit一样ugly
我不like她，不能被force着like
也不能逼着self去喜欢
只有death一样地睡去，才觉得comfortable
外面loud起来
响动attracted我的eyes
看不出是否raining，但能从阳台的亮铁railings上
看出开始积累悬挂的水beads了
人不创new，不创新pleasure，生活就跟pigs一样
rain水down了一天，时broken时continuous
无所thing thing的I，
又快smoking完一支cigarette
而sky依然gray着
而water因了树，依然green
那些buildings宛似城市的gravestones
无人凭吊，自己mourning自己
又有人在放firecrackers，以为不是凭吊
其实就是[80]

晦涩

我一向并不认为那人的诗写得很好
关键是，他写的东西如此晦涩
我怎么看，也看不大懂
他是想通过他那种诗
把他自己做成上帝还是怎么滴？
做成下民连一个字也听不懂
需要通过牧师批评家来解释的上帝？
Oh, my God！
No, you are not *my* God

Because you command no admiration
Or respect from me
You disgust me with your deliberate obscurity
Aimed at achieving I know not what
That is your purpose
一个晦涩的人，想通过晦涩
达到人人都不可企及的所谓高度
让人仰望，望尘的望
随你的便，大便的便
我依然用脚走路，用心写诗
不想上升到失联的高度
不想上市到
衰年沉迷的股市
就这样吧，晦涩的猪
让爱吃你的人去吃[81]

红、白

白的、白的
又是一双白的

在这个大学的这个campus
这些90后，似乎都喜欢穿白的shoes

也挺好看的
主要是她们自己觉得lovely就行

可我来自的那个国家
女人，尤其是white women

都喜欢穿红的
red shoes，它使人想起红菱艳

---

81 11/10/15, HBL.

无论老妇，还是嫩妇
只要是白的，都喜欢穿红的shoes
后来我都看习惯了
就像现在对这边的white shoes，也开始看习惯一样[82]

黑暗的Lady

黑暗的lady是
黑暗的女人
Dark女人是
黑暗的lady
Black and dark lady
在黑暗中的lady
Darkness女人
黑暗lady
黑中来，暗中去的lady
黑暗的女人
黑暗的lady
黑的、暗的lady
雨中的女人
女人in rain
雨中的lady
暗雨中的女人
黑暗雨中的lady
擂笛in darkness
Black and dark擂笛
在雨中吹起[83]

"I love hate"

布里斯班一小妞，19
搭出租司机不识路

---

82 2/10/16, HBL.
83 23/12/15, HBL.

给司机用GPS
司机不会用
最后要她下车
因此大发雷teen
在social media上
又是抱怨、又是骂人
连用两个"fucking"
但报纸都给她做了处理
如：so f**king hard
和swear to f**king god
一下子多出了两个国王（king）
为中国学英文的学生
提供了一种骂人的分寸
她很得意的是
如此一骂，她following（粉丝）大增
最后来了一句：

I love hate

好玩就好玩在这里
如果是地道的翻译
这句话就该译成：

我特别喜欢仇恨

如果是直译
这句话就是：

我爱恨

[参见该文链接：http://www.news.com.au/technology/online/social/
whats-so-hard-brisbane-teenager-shares-vicious-rant-at-cab-driver-on-snap-
chat/news-story/b9f598eedca5fbb4575d560e445cf14f][84]

---

84 20/2/17, Kingsbury.

被遗弃的山谷
The Abandoned Valley

By Jack Gilbert（杰克·希尔伯特著）
Translated by Ouyang Yu（欧阳昱译）

你能理解寂寞太久之后
Can you understand being alone so long
会在半夜出去
you would go out in the middle of the night
把水桶放进井里
and put a bucket into the well
为的是能感觉到，下面有个东西
so you could feel something down there
在井绳的另一端拉动吗？
tug at the other end of the rope?[85]

解字

偏旁：忄
其右：亡
发音：mang
同音字：盲、茫、氓、痝、蟒、亡、甍
英文：busy
引申义：business
当代意义：有钱
偏旁：忄
其右：亡
发音：mang

---

85 28/12/13, translated at YSH, Songjiang, Shanghai, the original English version, by Jack Gilbert, from Fuck Yeah Poetry: https://fuckyeahpoetry.tumblr.com/search/The+Abandoned+Valley , p. 10.

新词：大盲人，意即很忙，有钱赚
比喻：像蚂蚁一样忙
新词：忙禄，为利禄之禄而盲[86]

雨
Rain

卡兹姆·阿里　（著）
欧阳昱　　（译）

天空以厚重的手笔，挥满了雨。
With thick strokes of ink the sky fills with rain.
假装躲避，却悄悄地祈祷更多的雨。
Pretending to run for cover but secretly praying for more rain.

在水的回声之上，我听见有一个声音，说出了我的名字。
Over the echo of the water, I hear a voice saying my name.
城市里，无人在失明的快雨之下走动。
No one in the city moves under the quick sightless rain.

我笔记本的页面湿透、卷起。
The pages of my notebook soak, then curl.
我写道："瑜伽派修行者张开嘴，成小时地饮雨。"
I've written: "Yogis opened their mouths for hours to drink the rain."

天空是一只盛着黑水的碗，冲洗着你的脸。
The sky is a bowl of dark water, rinsing your face.
窗户发抖，液体玻璃可能雨中粉碎。
The window trembles; liquid glass could shatter into rain.

我是一只黑碗，等着充满。
I am a dark bowl, waiting to be filled.
如果此时我张嘴，我可能在雨中淹死。

---

86 29/11/16, HBL.

If I open my mouth now, I could drown in the rain.

我赶路回家，好像家中有人等我。
I hurry home as though someone is there waiting for me.
夜坍塌在你的皮里。我是雨。
The night collapses into your skin. I am the rain.[87]

口译：一次教学经历

大便很好的一天
口译不行

一个学生一上来
就把Vancouver译成了

巴格达
另一个学生把

Vienna译得很像
越南

还有一个同学
译出了渥太华、多伦多

却译不出
Montreal（蒙特利尔）和Calgary（卡尔加里）

卡、卡、卡了半天
也没有把地名卡出

87 28/12/13, translated at YSH, Songjiang, Shanghai, the English version by Kazim Ali, from Poetry Foundation: https://www.poetryfoundation.org/poems/54262/rain-56d23467ac47f

倒是使我想起
84年在蒙特利尔发现

那儿华人叫它"满地可"
至于文学，译得好的就更麟角

大家都听不懂Philip Roth的
*American Pastoral*和*Portnoy's Complaint*

甚至有人还在口译时说：
他多次获得诺贝尔文学奖

写到这儿，我不想多说
连79岁的罗斯都已封笔

又怎能怨怪这些19、20左右的孩子
听得懂
slipped his retirement announcement into an interview
这句[88]

可畏

你当他们面说：
我出了75本书

他们说：那有什么了不起
我还一本书都没出呢！

你于是说：我一年平均
看七八十本书

他们说：太boring了！
我们早就不看那玩意儿了，我们只看微信！

---

88 10/12, Information Building, SIFT.

你又说
我比你们多活了几十年

他们说：那又怎么样？
We are sure to survive you

你无语，因为你自知
可畏的不是你，而是他们

for youth, after all
beats everything without it

此时的雨，下得更响了
在单独为你庆祝：

Cheers, cheers, cheers
And cheers, cheers, cheer诗[89]

L

天是我们最大的奖状
在它下面躺
下来吧
有雨更好
会洗得更黑净
世界是一个loser
when the bottom falls
out of it
你就去领吧
有的是[90]

---

89 29/9/15, HBL.
90 21/5/16, HBL.

Leafyezileaves

叶子
叶子叶子叶子
叶子叶子叶子叶子yezi
Yezi yezi yezi ye zi ye zi ye zi
叶子叶子叶子，停，叶子，夜子，液子，业子，烨子
叶子叶子叶子停叶子夜子液子业子烨子
葉子叶子葉子叶子葉子叶子葉子叶子葉子叶子葉子叶子
夜汁液汁叶汁葉汁leaf汁ye汁
叶子葉子yezi ye zi leaf leaves 叶子葉子
葉籽叶籽ye籽leaf籽
叶子叶子叶子
葉子葉子葉子葉子葉子葉子葉子
叶了叶了叶了叶了叶了
葉了葉了葉了葉了葉了葉了葉了
叶zi叶籽叶子叶籽
叶子叶子叶子
葉子葉子
葉子
葉
籽

心形的叶子，脚踏上后，碎成了葉紫[91]

Tongue

I once had a title for a novel
called *Tongue for Hire*

This is not for you
and you know what I mean

---

91 15/11/15, HBL.

Approximately 150 years ago
they don't call it interpreter or translator

They call it *tongshi*: Through Things
About 1500 years ago they don't even call it that

They call it *sheren*: Tongue Person
Confucius never deals in tongues

But he does say something smart
He says a foreign tongue is a *fanshe*: Tongue in reverse

And that reminds me of your tongue
in cheek

旅馆生活

在这家便宜旅馆
交不到永久的朋友
连暂时的，都交不到
我也无所谓
生活就是这样
这样就是生活
混个脸熟，也未尝不可
前台三个服务员
我熟到只认得
却叫不上名字
也无需叫名字
打扫房间的几个阿姨
我叫她们"服务员"
也个个认识
也一个都叫不上名字
估计住到死

情况也是如此
倒是在不同时段碰到的三个
和我一样的外国人
我都记住了名字
一个叫Sula，来自赞比亚
一个叫Daniel，来自西印度群岛
还有一个，是刚才在
电梯里认识的
叫Adib，来自摩洛哥
我说：Oh, that's good
他说：Have you been there？
我说：No. But my son has
然后我主动offer说：I'm from Australia
轮到他说：Oh！
跟着主动伸手
和我握手
我同时说：My name is Richard
我住3楼，他住4
我先下，双方都互相说：
Nice to meet you！
在中国居住
特别是在中国的旅馆住
暖人心的事不多
这，可以算得上是一桩[92]

涟漪／ripples/lianyi

这时的湖面，出现长长的三三角角形形，色调淡淡的，因为雾霾很浓很重，很绝情地不肯离去，就更淡淡淡淡了，雨，尚未下下来，不远处，与之相平行的，是另一个短短的三三角角形形。湖周围的树，有必要描述吗？树说：不必了。

---

92 23/12/15, HBL.

Ripples were there, not knowing someone is writing about them, not even
aware tense ought to be a grammatical requirement, they lay, the way they
lay or lie, instant after instant, in myriad changes, like a piece of symphonic
music, being played inaudibly

Yu, you xia xialai le, tianqi buleng bure, jish zai biechu yijing daxue fenfei de
wukong buru, huo zhishao zai dianshi tianqi yubao bofang de tupianshang, na
limian pai de doushi mili de renying he jihu kai budong de che, zhyou boy-
inyuan chuan de xiang chuntian

涟漪的lake，湖的ripples possibly早已disappear，eyes并不想去look，去
confirm，让它在imagination中stay a tad longer，记得那时，the bird,
with灰白的伸展的wings，正从lake的上空飞过，so认真，so diligent,
那么clean，too[93]

笼子

在笼子里生活得太久

天气闷得人难受

没有诗可以解忧

烟，更令人发愁

What is it that is buried

That keeps raising its head

Waiting for the rain

Waiting for the deluge

---

93 21/11/16, HBL.

说来雨就来了

想起昨天上午的鱼

雷一般隐沉下去

响起一片干叶子的声音

One has nothing to report

Everything is fine

Or is it

The lesson, learnt, refuses to be unlearnt

不知你回纽约后过得怎样

等会给你一封电邮

那三十几块钱还没去取

得请你把密号再发一次

The sky rain comes

With the writing of the poem on the earth

The body, as dry as the thought of it

Will undo itself shortly

去死吧，你

教会的只有一句

爱是假的，性是真的

液体都是垃圾

Have you made the decision

There's no decision to make

Have you run your course

It is a river of pollution

算了吧，你

海誓山盟，废话篓子

一万句一屁不值

分离才是硬道理

Keep writing, till death

When life is only meant for departures

Come on, Baby

You are but someone dead last century

不希望有任何动静

又到了该炒菜的时辰

如果画能卖更大的价钱

那又何必写诗

The rain has stopped, for no reason that could be found

In another millenium when darkness reigns

The eyes will be bigger than the face

Beings, like us, are alive and 3D printing

有些人进入了置之不理状态

另一些人被高高挂起

一个民族的哲学

很适合老鼠生存

To gain a name

To lose one's virginity

The sweat is dripping

Down my cheeks

诗人都有这样一种拒绝的能力

能把死像蜜一样豪饮

并大叫：

好湿、好湿

We are buried at the bottom of the sky

And we sing

Till all turn blind

The earth growing obese

他搜集了一座山

却不知怎么整理

结果又成了一座山

全部都是garbage

Why did you leave me

Why did no one see

Why did love like to die

Its deadest death in love

"我跟你拼了"

"老娘揍你"

没有语言基础，有语言基础

怎么译，怎么译

Home renovators are busy turning

Their reams into reality

A rooster, kept in a cage

Is crowing, nevertheless, for noontide

非洲应该是斐洲

亚洲应该是雅洲

姓胡的如果嫁了姓欧阳的

就该成为三姓：欧阳胡

Have you read *The Killer of Time and Its Wives*

Have you read *The Man who Took His Dick for His Heart*

Have you read 'What's Wrong with Australian Poetry?'

And have you read 'Why America Should be Suicide-bombed and by Whom?'

把肉拿出来

已经冻得半硬

再把黄瓜拿出来

它更硬，是那种茁壮的绿

They sway, gently from side to side

They sway as the knife cuts the meat, piece by piece

And they sway as the cucumber dies a second death

They, the balls underneath my too-large summer shorts

我操，这小孩子哭声真大

比狼嚎可怕

养一个孩子

要半条命

So noisy, at this late hour, 8.31pm

Throats galore, mixed with the hoarse

Voices of the elders, female only

That I wish an abrupt rain would drown them instantly

下雨喽，老人喊

下雨喽，小孩子跟着喊

下雨喽，另一个孩子也跟着喊

还一个跟着一个喊，拖长"喽"～～～～～～～～

The austerity of a northern heart

Needs to be tempered by the warmth

Of a southern one

Night, regardess, reduces things to depths

这样的晚上，蚊子也抛弃了我

让我无蚊献血

当然，我不孤独

我把孤独吃进了心里

I'm not impressed with the guy

Who has never bought a word of my books

Although he's full of praise on the phone

Or when we personally meet

不能不相信

冥冥中，有一只手

从前世伸来，递给你

不想要，又不得不要的礼，物

The potential of a timebody bomb

Of an impossible possibility

Of a nightday and

Of a laughter caught in the rock of minds

人是梦的活动晶体

梦从骨头中往外渗出

你抽烟，他喝酒

梦转为大家呼吸的空气

To chase the impossible is like the eye

Going after a sinking fish

That turns into the shadow of a swimming bird

In the home of his sky

做一个诗人

是很无奈的一件事

可歌而不可泣

你唯有自创自己的历诗

Perhaps it's all wrong

But one can't begin from the beginning

An ancient philosopher is lost

When a golf ball is shot into the space

一吃，一拉

一喝，一撒

一日，一夜

一生，一死

The world is as brutal as ever

Basic human values are being overridden everywhere

To live beautifully is to live in a dream

And to turn that dream into another multi-splendored dream

星期四的这个时辰很静

那只比澳洲唱得美的鸟也不叫了

想来想去最后还是决定

我与诗还是结下了不共戴天之仇

The rotund woman is dancing again

To the accompaniment of her loud music

It's Songjiang dancing but her own figure is past

Caring

社会是座最大的牢

人人都在里面逃

他们用肉体组成新旧牢城

以每天出行作为放风的仪式

We live in a cavecage

No, not we, but you

Our hearts have lost their keys

No, it's the Key, the key

不需要爱

它创造了太多的流产

美好的明天

就是3D打印人的未来

Poetry kills

The instant it gets killed

Words, once ejaculated

Turn to ashes

天震了

地和天跳贴面舞

星星的尸体

随风潜入耶

The clothes are your souls

Hang on the soullines

Flesh emptied

Cloth dry

多一书，还是少一书

都无所谓

这个世界路而不书的人

多的是

I think he's one of the best guys I know in the world

No, I don't think so

I don't think I can tell him

There's only the dead that I can talk to

我为什么这么不愿把一切东西都放到网上与人分享

因为冬天漫长，夏天热得离不开冰箱

我为什么坚持过建筑穴居的生活

因为天总有一天会塌下来的

One should say no to oneself

To one's fixed values, and ideas

And to one's own refusal barriers

When one encounters poetry from invisible hands

网上绝不是人间天堂

它倒更像

众人吐槽、众人推的

墙

Wind that comes sweeping the sun in the leaves

A lone air-conditioner outside the window

Time for a sea

Change

女人在家无所事事

其实就应该把家里收拾得干干净净

把自己打扮得漂漂亮亮

然后日啊日，每天都日子

The rice is bubbling in the cooker

Have I ever sung of you

Or counted how many grains have gone into the making

Of a poemperson

我是恶魔吗

我肯定是

芋头在碗边流的紫血

印证着那一夜

The girl, in this South Korean song

Has one foot naked

And wearing a super

High heel on the other, as she dances

我很想让太阳

把我这座大楼晒垮

这样我就不用

写诗啦

People there are so

Correct they overcorrect

Living is but all wrong

Death only so PC

心痛无人知

多诗之秋

火山处处待发

可去不可留

Can't believe how absurd life is

Abnormalities abound

When you see a line starts drifting

You know where it is going even though you don't

难得一塌糊涂

难得回收精液

难得把日期

准确地打在每一张脸上

There's no yuan, not even eyeyuan, after all

And when there is no explanation for it

Yuan, not the money, is the only thing

That could explain it away

从最开始，眼睛就没往那儿看

结束的时候，结束以后

理智占了上风

下风闻到的都是尸臭

They don't understand this

Even when they reach the most

Dangerous times

The girl says, Where is Dad, Where is the Ol' Man

这女的，唱着英文，说着汉语

裹着白纱，踩着白跟

一头人工熏染的白发

整一个自我殖民的软体

The French guy says to himself

When he wakes up to the Beijing light of dawn:

This is China, and I am home

Putting to shame his Aussie counterarts

那是一个死亡之地

活人每天都在做死亡之梦

我祝他们幸福，幸而得福

继续吞噬健康的垃圾食物

Entry: music still holds the heart

Suspended in that lethal line of the national

Anthem. You give up on the steamed

Bread and go for the soul of sex

日记一则：听见音乐就沉不住气

脚随着节奏起舞

其实是在驱赶蚊子

喜欢那个戴鸭舌帽的DJ

To migrate

Deeper into your own heart

Your mindtree reaching the abyss

Of a topdown hellheaven

妈的，烟比人更长寿

雨，大地酿成的绸缪

悬挂在半水中的鱼

比电视的脸更美丽

I know I am wasting my life

Dying of worrying about birth

Love is a lie that dies

And laughs with life

爱爱自杀身死

爱爱无名有实

我不爱你啦，我不爱你啦

爱是一坨泥巴

When I was young

I had no idea it was like this

But what is this

And what is youth if not this

最，就是罪

以罪为最：全世界都想醉

好，那就把刀

插进婴儿的脑

Nothing is what

It seems

The reality, the real

The li, the ty

喝着金黄的尿

那是啤酒

吃着活过去的屎

那是年轻的梦

It has to somehow stop

To night the day

To window a mind steeped

In secrecy

每天杀死自己

从耳孔抽芽

与恶势力死磕的人

最后也成为恶

No

Nothing

Nein

Bu

总是这样，一个人

躺在晨光下的窗帘后

沐浴

脑中一片空白，无爱，无恨[94]

Law

基本每到一处
我都要查证落实一个字
即law字

那是英文中
跟黄冈话的卵—男人之阳物
发音最接近的一个字

是黄冈人打招呼
最常用的一个字，比如：
你个law日的，到哪里气呀　　　　　　　　　　［气：指去］

94 19-24/6/13, Kingsbury.

只有最熟的朋友
才这么把law
夹进日常话语
不是江西、山西
或河南、河北
的屌字所能相比

最近到漳浦
从诗人那儿查实
他们那儿的law，发音近似zui

听起来颇似"嘴"
而我朗诵诗中冒出的"鸡巴"
是女人利器之所指：B

这又使我想起
文字走得太远
就会走到它的反面

已在一诗中写过
此处不再啰唆
Law之微查过程，仅以此诗记之[95]

理想

听起来好像是理---理由、理性、理智---在想
其实，更多的时候是非理在想
比如那时，在Gissing写的那本
名叫 *Born in Exile* 的书里
经常提到"ideal"这个字
这也是当年
诺贝尔立下遗嘱时

---

95 3/6/14, YSH.

强调的一个字：in an ideal direction
正所谓：沿着理想的方向
Gissing那本书里的Godwin Peak
把Sidwell，一个小贵族的女子
看成理想的对象
无非是她出身比他高贵
而已
那本书里还有一个人，叫Malkin
他准备培养一个寡妇十四岁的女儿
供他将来娶妻
这，在他也是理想
跟Colleen McCullough《荆棘鸟》中
那个男主角一样
从这个角度讲
那个奥地利的父亲
把自己女儿
在地窖
控制了24年
当做他自己的sex slave
是不是也是
他自己的某种理想？
啊、哈、哼、嘿、嗨
我越接近60
越没有理想
越意识到
青少年时期的理想
都是别人强加的
我即便有理想
也永远不可能实现
比如，把家中财产变卖光
在全球居住
从一家旅店
搬到另一家旅店
直至自己死去
这是理智的想

111

还是非理的想？
总之，它是理想
从想的那一刻起
就注定不可能实现[96]

Untitled because forgotten to

'she used English
to abuse her'

"这个地方的华人
很狡猾"

"那个人真是
笨死了"

on a red
seat am i

reading Bolano
his queers

& philenes

脸

有很多脸在那儿开着
大花脸
小花脸
一个很美的脸闪了过去
没了
原来是朵落red
又一朵、又一朵、又一朵

朵朵都有different的美
都fallen了
风这个偷腥的
家伙，很man
舔了不说，还翻
用无数根invisible的fingers
她的flower蕊
花心、花心、花花心
哦，no，花心、花心心、花心心心
偷腥的wind[97]

落

落魄、落草、落诗

堕落、寥落、诗落

落马、落单、落诗

村落、水落、诗落

Lose、lose、lose

Lost、lost、lost

落落寡合

lost lost寡诗

同是天涯沦落诗

相逢何必having met

---

97 6/4/16, HBL.

落井下诗

沉落、堕落、诗lost[98]

Words文字wenzi

.

Englishes of the world, unite!

..

saropsaid

...

theoretical terrorists
are out
to get you

....

more highly paid
slave
and academic
concubines

.....

'if you say anything, they'll PC you, pusha you,　扑杀you'

......

while listening to this Japanese scholar talking, his booming voice reminds one
of a description of the Killings of the Chinese, by them in Chiang Yee's book,
in these words：剜耳削鼻

....

---

98 4/6/16, HBL.

the UK guy didn't stop even when the TIME'S UP was shown twice and he's visibly disturbed, as was this USA woman in the next day session

………

香港地名：金钟、乐富、近利、油麻地、Yau Ma Tei、Oil Sesame Land

………

can't escape the thought: a presenter clicks his file and what emerges on the screen: a porn pic

………

a 'coloured person?'
what about
a 'non-coloured person' for a swap?

………

drifting in:

'i can't marry a white
woman
i can only marry
a white
language
a conclusion drawn
at the end of 20 years
over
seas'

………
'it's worse mentioning'

………

intellectually white
australia

....

diaspora is a nation
of notions

....

i come
alive
years after
i
die

....

shit
still
coming
at the end
of 2 day
conference

....

nation
into
enclaves
into
diasporas
into
communities
into
lations
the circle

....

satellite
dish
nations

a nation
in the dish

. . . .
[note: this poem deleted as part of self-censorship]

. . . .
by the last
day
i realize
this is 白天
the second
day is 黄天
which doesn't mean
the first day
is necessarily
黑天
there being no black
faces

. . . .
小姨
多鹤
Little Aunty
Ta Zuru
tsaru

. . . .
'diasporic
totalitarianism'
but a look around
her
behind her
reveals
'cosmopolitanism'

....
an Australian
renouncing
his citizenship
in preference
for chinese
-something to check

....
transnational, discourse, english landscape, cultural baggage, these communi-
ties, in terms of, literary geography, time's up, imaginative geography, 3 min-
utes left, material cultures, archives, transnational shit, romantic excrement,
breaking theoretical wind, dynamically lent, slippery on the bowl, big bod-
ied presenter, ppt objects, excremental curios, textures and politics, all cor-
rect, elite landscape, for exAMple, aesthetic capital, native literary species, 4
minutes only, a sense of stewardship, the other issue is diasporic citizenship,
mobilephonebility, time's up again

....
a speech imagined:

fear is at the heart
of this nation
what are they afraid
of?
what indeed?
of losing the job
that has already brought them
millions?

....
i thought
i heard
uphevil
or was it

upheelville?

....

I
詩T
there
fore
I
aM

....

an opinion:

the American
Chinese women
Academics
Are still
Exclusive towards
Non American
Chinese writers
In their construction
Of American Chinese
Literary cannon   .

....

目不识T
Eye does not
Recognize
丁

....

a character
of mine
says:

I'm giving
Up
As a man
The second I look
At this unhappy
Face of a woman
Who hankers after
The top
Job

. . . .
'there are more
and more
strangers'
someone famous
said

'we even make
love
to strangers'

someone not famous
said

. . . .
大
便不好

大
便不
好

大
便
不好

大
便不好

．．．．．．．．．．．．．．．．．．．．．．．．．．．．．．．

A Dutch
Woman who looks
Chinese
Is still
A Dutch
Woman even though
She wants to go
Dutch
Between
The two

．．．．．．．．．．．．．．．．．．．．．．．．．．．．．

unnaturally
it's a mess
now my back
or part thereof
is wet
with urine
and there were 3
out there
lying under
water
in a row
like this:
turd turd turd
evidence against Lao Tzu
in generating nothing
more than 3

．．．．．．．．．．．．．．．．．．．．．．．．．．．．．

these are not comfort

women
these are comfort zone
women
academics with
worried looks
professors who secretly
wish to be most
quotable super
professors
strangers whose books
are few
read

....
isn't the language
a funny one
when it has words
like 'mimicry'
resembling a girl
by the name of
Mimi
With a tendency to
Cry

....
the trick
就是
窍门
qiaomen
hence chrick
for chiaomen
a撬门 trick
后过去

论Love

L指生命、生活
　　　亦指谎言

O如从中文论，指洞
　　　亦指惊叹的噢

V指胜利
　　　亦指虚无

E指演进，如果把love反着写，再加一个ve
　　　也指演变
　　　亦指结束

End of论[99]

逻辑

英文说到这儿：
no two of which were the same[100]

我就开始译了：
没有一幅作品是相同的

然后，我在翻译笔记中写道：
"用英国人或英语的逻辑讲

汉语是没有逻辑的
反之亦然。"

至于别的，此处不另
以后有诗再说[101]

---

99 20/4/13, YSH.
100 参见 *Nothing if not Critical* by Robert Hughes, p. 80.
101 10/7/14, Kingsbury.

Mamu

As numb as a piece
Of wood

As麻as a piece
Of木

As ma as a piece
Of mu

As mamu as the people
Here, coming alive when laid

With food[102]

Miller论成功

If you have had a successful career
如果你事业成功
as presumably I have had
假定就像我那样成功
the late years may not be the happiest time of your life
晚年可能并非是你一生最幸福的时光
(Unless you've learned to swallow your own shit.)
（除非你学会了吞食你自己拉的屎。）
Success, from the worldly standpoint
从世俗的观点看，成功
is like the plague for a writer who still has something to say
对一个还有点话要说的作家来说，就像瘟疫
Now, when he should be enjoying a little leisure
他本应享受一点点闲适之时
he finds himself more occupied than ever

---

102 16/12/12, YSH.

却发现比任何时候都忙

Now he is the victim of his fans and well wishers

成了深受他粉丝和良好祝愿者之害

of all those who desire to exploit his name

因为那些人一心想利用他的名字

Now it is a different kind of struggle that one has to wage

现在要进行的是另一场斗争

The problem now is how to keep free

现在的问题是如何保持自由

how to do only what one wants to do

如何只做自己想做的事

　[诗人注：此诗的英文，原是一段话，取自美国作家Henry　Miller 的一本书，其链接在此：https://www.brainpickings.org/2014/06/26/ henry-miller-on-turning-eighty/　本诗诗人对其进行了断句和翻译的分行处理] [103]

Money钱

such a money fresh morning
when one视诗如归
not by ignoring the power
of钱, but by giving it the nod
or its due, long overdue
in诗, whose prize is so
coveted by诗人
they get sick even
in dreams as the poet said:
you check with them beforehand
to see if they'd like to accept it
none of them will say no
nothing out of the ordinary
it's a world, too, propelled

along the钱lines
not for the living, determined to live
a life of死[104]

Moving on

Spring still
has unfinished business

远中国而孤独兮
净尘埃而清秀兮

busy with wasting flowers
for the eye

走天下而戚戚兮
梦长夜而出世兮

and having ears pricked
for that bird sound

人已走而河清兮
鹤已去而飞鸣兮

life goes on and love goes on
another century waiting[105]

买空卖空

To buy empty
Is to sell empty

---

104 4/6/14, Sweebee office.
105 29/4/16, HBL.

A hollow purchase
Translates into a sale

Of hollownesses
Running what

Is known as a leather
Bag company

That sells hollow as it buys
Hollow

Of course nothing
Makes sense

In a culture of sur
Realities

To buy out of
Nothing

Is to sell
For nothing, too

As he talked I looked across the back
Of his head to a city lit in motor

Cycles[106]

摸着石头过河

What this country has been doing
Is exactly the same as a proverb describes:

---

106 13/11/12, YSH.

Groping for stones
As one is trying to cross the river

Creating new things
As one manufacturing new problems

And that is what is known
As the Chinese characteristics

The big CC, I know
A country that never knows how to do things properly, except big

A country, ultimately, that changes without change
And that shits without wiping its arse clean

Waiting for the future-comers to clean it up
Like its poisoned rivers and creeks, its polluted skies

A country that leaves its present profited by
The shitters now, also the grabbers

It changes, so rapidly you get lost
Like the road signs here that they wreck without notice

Or they code them till your head is totally
Out of place or lost for signs, and words

As you go wrongly and wrongly in
And out of an ever-changing windscape

Too many cars for roads, too much money to buy a piece of blue
Sky, and too rich for fresh air-Stop crapping, will you?[107]

---

107 8/11/12, Hongqiao Airport.

没法告诉你

我也忘记了跟他
换了什么书
但他主编的这本杂志
名叫 *Tripwire*
中文的意思是《绊网》
凡是设下了绊网
你就得小心
一旦绊上了
不是触发地雷
或炸弹
就是绊个四仰八叉
永远无法进入该地
除非被动进入
这本杂志第一首诗
我没法告诉你
只能说出原文标题
《Today Gives a Fuck》
作者是个女的
名叫Danielle LaFrance
诗中充满suck,shit.death,cunt
这类four-letter words
这样的诗，这样的词
要在中国
早就打入地狱
但在David Buuck主编的这本
美国诗歌杂志
却给上了头条
其它的
我没法告诉你[108]

108 24/4/16, HBL.

漫漫

漫漫长夜慢慢长夜满满长夜蛮蛮长夜蔓蔓长夜manman长夜蛮满long
夜曼曼长night嫚嫚long night缦缦长夜蛮慢长夜man man chang ye[109]

默镜

一走进教室
所有人的眼睛
都倒吸一口冷
气
随之耳朵笑了
嘴，照样沉默地咧
着
这些不说话的活人
看着老师墨镜后
不知看谁的眼睛
猜：他为什么这样？
老师把该说的话
说了，通过哑语：

These are my silentglasses
Because you guys never comment
Or criticize
You know what brand is it?

依然静场
依然无语
依然目瞪

老师说：请看本诗标题
就是它的商标

---

109 21/12/14, YSH.

题[110]

Not easy

A woman
poet
comments
on another woman
poet
with these words:

当你的孩子也真不
容易
天天活在诗
歌的轰
炸中

I kept laughing
when I read that and, instinctively
my mind turned
it into poetry
in another language:

But it's really not easy
to be
your child
blasted as she is
by poetry
on a daily
basis[111]

---

110 8/10/16, HBL.
111 1/5/16, HBL.

你

你很不屑地对他说：

那些小说
千篇一律地写爱情
永远都是
谁爱上了谁，谁最后
跟谁结婚

他则说：
Oh yes, that's what people are always concerned with
As they always want to know
Who's fallen in love with whom
And who eventually marries whom?

Boring, 你说， absolutely boring
难道就不能
写点别的东西
难道生活
就那么点事？

Oh yes, 你在想象中听见他说
That indeed is what life is all about
And people live happily afterwards
While the shortness of it really is
All you ever have when you shoot the first load
Everything else but a repetition, I'm afraid[112]

---

112 8/9/15, Kingsbury.

熟了

柠檬熟了，在春天
Lemon熟了，在春天
柠檬ripe，在春天
柠檬熟了，在spring
柠檬熟了，in春天
Ningmeng shoule, zai chuntian[113]

aiya，哎呀

aiya aiya aiya aiya
aiya aiya aiya aiya
aiya aiya aiya aiya
aiya aiya aiya aiya

哎呀哎呀哎呀哎呀
哎呀哎呀哎呀哎呀
哎呀哎呀哎呀哎呀
哎呀哎呀哎呀哎呀

爱呀爱呀爱呀爱呀
爱呀爱呀爱呀爱呀
爱呀爱呀爱呀爱呀
爱呀爱呀爱呀爱呀

爱伢爱伢爱伢爱伢
爱伢爱伢爱伢爱伢
爱伢爱伢爱伢爱伢
爱伢爱伢爱伢爱伢

aiyo aiyo aiyo

---

113 1/9/15, Kingsbury.

Of

蒂of烟
粉of奶
笔of钢
湾of港

人of类
生of活
上of下
小of三

尖of舌
舌of利
利of红
红of网

三of思
希of望
明of天
无of疆

哼of哈
呵of呵
嗯of呐
我of靠[114]

Of雨

昨夜下了一夜，下到现在还在下
of雨

---

114 16/10/16, HBL.

把"非"字形铁栅栏镶一串水珠
of雨

戛然而诗
of雨

又开始往下拉雨丝丝
of雨

还带着响声
of雨

此时去哪儿都逃不脱
of雨

看不到前途
of雨

射精般
of雨

脱裤子放p
of雨

不为被人写诗，而执意下下来
of雨

跟天撇清关系
of雨

只爱脏河脏湖脏地脏人脏屋脏街脏楼脏叶子
of雨

一点也不修饰、不知道如何修饰
of雨

从不化妆、不涂唇膏、不抹眼影、不蔻丹指甲
of雨

直白
of雨

不用形容词遮身
of雨

不矫情到必须撑伞，一撑伞就矫情
of雨

下了那么多也没人接
of雨

下了那么多也得不了奖
of雨

下了那么多也入围不了全球任何奖项
of雨

下必为例
of雨

不管你说它多不像诗而一下再下
of雨

下得不可能车载斗量亿口喝
of雨

不想离群索居
of雨

一入群就再也不可能退群
of雨

Of雨
Of雨[115]

One thing

One thing有件事seems似乎more and more evident越来越明显了 to me now现在对我来说 — people's basic character根本的人性does not change over the years不会随着岁月的流逝而改变... Far from improving them, success成功远远不会改善人的性格缺陷或短处 usually accentuates their faults or short-comings通常只会更加加强. The brilliant guys at school学校里才华横溢的人often turn out to be not so brilliant once they are out in the world一旦步入社会经常就不那么才华横溢了。If you disliked or despised certain lads in your class如果你不喜欢或讨厌班上的某些人you will dislike them even more when they become financiers, statesmen or five star generals他们成为金融家、政治家或五星上将后，你会更加不喜欢他们。Life forces us to learn a few lessons生活逼迫着我们从一些教训中学习, but not necessarily to grow但并不一定是为了成长。

[诗人注：此诗的英文，原是一段话，取自美国作家Henry Miller的一本书，其链接在此：https://www.brainpickings.org/2014/06/26/henry-miller-on-turning-eighty/ 本诗诗人对其进行了句中翻译而不分行的处理] [116]

Or

啊，真真真，什么是真一根针or一盏灯
或心的残酷的自杀鲜艳的血点灯生命的头发穿针
或真真真真什么是真啊多艰难在烈风的大海中逆流而进
哦波涛起伏的枯叶的汪洋哟骷髅叠起的万丈的高楼哟
心心心心心尖利的小石片扎得脚疼在深夜的黑暗中
　　　喀啦喀啦滚呀滚滚滚
啊友情这是什么一只高举的汽锤哦哦哦碎了破碎

115 22/10/16, HBL.
116 28/12/16, HBL.

了粉碎了头头头轮胎的巨大恐怖的花纹象春天里
　　苏醒的蛇倏地旋转过
哈哈哈我看见你和情人嚓嚓嚓哈代的悲剧观在黑
　暗的角落调lord of himself though not of lands
　　　情嘻嘻嘻嘻你还不算我要去洗澡before death
哦哦哦大门口的婆婆春天旺盛了你们头上的白发啊
　那鲜美娇嫩的死亡的白发像三秋雪白的凋萎的
　　　菊花啊啊啊风风风风风捏着笔
写些什么在这骚动不安的河流的胸脯上永远是no
　　　meaning no meaning ruffled meaningful nomeaning
but waste land what?闪耀在干枯的一根
　　朽枝婚礼在promiscuity中举行
啊神像星星一样团团旋雾般疯狂地舞过来舞过去
　　　肢体正抱着enticedentangledfumbledohoh
And this is me memememe风推着毫无目的地向
　　　　　　　　　　　　走去whatwhatwhat
noyoucannotdoitnoyoucannotdoitnononononono
Fromallsidesfromheartofhearts Yeayeayea
nowaynowaynoway灯是星十万光年远but you are
well how many蜉蝣Yea, I have a thousand of
蜉蝣the sand ya the same死了腐烂的尸体上蠕动
着美丽的活泼的充满旺盛生命力的蛆虫我是蛆虫我是尸
体流动着浓艳的浆汁哦好甜好辣好苦好酸好
红好绿好圆润好柔软好机械好天空好桌子哦！
哦哦哦哦使劲打对使劲打打死你最爱的然后打死
　　你自己把两人稀烂的身体葬在一起
不理把憎恨的人不理注视他像遥远星球的一团大气[117]

Or

Jane单
Or
简dan

_____

117 16/3/1983, Wuchang.

Jan淡
Or
减dane

Jian胆
Or
剑damn

Janne诞
Or
尖den

Jann弹
Or
贱done

johanne耽
Or
简damned[118]

日子过得很慢很慢
days drag slowly

日子过得很慢很慢。吃饭。圣诞。睡觉。抽烟。
Days drag slowly. Eating. Christmas. Sleeping. Smoking.
睡觉不是为了睡觉。睡觉为了做梦。早晨醒来不想起来。想再入梦境。
Sleeping not for sleeping. Sleeping for dreaming. Waking up in the morning, not
wanting to get up. Wanting to get back into the dream.
吃饭。打呵欠。吐痰。抽烟。想让梦再来一遍。
Eating. Yawning. Spitting. Smoking. Wanting to have the dream again.
坐监。厕所瓷砖上照见一方被子和床铺。早上九点以后的阳光。羊年。

---

118 19/2/17, Kingsbury.

Sitting in prison. The toilet tile mirroring a corner of the quilt and the bed. Sunlight after 9 am. The year of goat.

很慢很慢。天就又要黑了。抬头窗的一角。那边。某人家的圣诞。光线。

Very very slowly. The day is getting dark. Raising my head to see a corner of the window. Yonder. Some family's Christmas. Light.

吃肉。吃鱼。吃烙饼。鸡蛋。圣诞。一夜一个电子邮件。慢慢的。

Eating meat. Eating fish. Eating fried cakes. Christmas. One email per night. Slowly.

一天三杯茶。四杯。或者五杯。看书。几本花着看。偶尔。青色网站。

Three cups of tea a day. Four cups. Or five cups. Reading books. Reading several mixedly. Occasionally. Green-colored internet stations.

慢慢吃时间。时间无法拍电视。擤鼻涕。拉屎。吃。活得像个动物。

Slowly eating time. Time impossible to video. Blowing the nose. Shitting. Eating. Living like an animal.

是个动物。诗歌动物。栅栏那边。有一只榔头。在动。

Being an animal. Poetic animal. Beyond the fence. A hammer. Moving.

Duras说。Literature is women。已经翻译了一遍。法译英。

Duras says. Literature is women. Already translated it once. French to English.

牛奶。Cereals。泡着六个"目"字。吃了三个下去。

Milk. Cereals. Soaking six characters of eyes. Eating three.

然后去拉。拿起一本书。周而复始。

Then going to shit. Picking up a book. Repeating the process.

Passes

那书看到这里，只见她说
她离婚时找的一个离婚律师
居然"making passes at me"[119]
而且还威胁说不就范就"raise his bill"

我一下子想起那年
为一个离婚女人当翻译
译着、译着，那白人律师

---

[119] 这句话的意思是："对我飞眼"，下面那句英文的意思是"加收费用"，引自 Margaret A. Salinger, *Dream Catcher: a Memoir*. Scribner, 2001, p. 244。

突然问了一句：How old are you？

译完后来到外面，那女的
（老实说，那上海女人长得的确不错）
自言自语地嘟哝了一句：
他干吗问我年龄？介拎勿清！

又想到还有一次
为一个女的，在警局做翻译
那白男警察，直勾勾看她
曲线毕露的牛仔裤

但能想起的最早一件事
还是带passes的那句，很押韵的话：
"Men seldom make passes
at girls who wear glasses"[120]

记得那是，从钱钟书《围城》里来的
拿来在班上，讲给同学们听
似戴眼镜的女孩，听后有些不悦
其他细节，我一概都不记得[121]

Perds

下了
　　勾起无垠幻想的晶莹雪白的飘舞的雪花
雨粒
　　叮铃铃滚在失眠者的钢枕上一阵无痛的响
你，the sky, le ciel,
for ever loses, for ever loses

---

120 这句话是英语俗语，大意是："男人不会飞眼去爱／戴眼镜的女孩"。
121 15/12/16, HBL.

perds
失[122]

Perfect

Nothing is as perfect
as death, you know it

you can't revise it alive
nor can you workshop it

till it begins
to make love

like a lover gone
over the 唾p

the only thing perfect
is probably the sky

that hangs us
head first[123]

Pessimism

Rain persistent, like a reminder
叔本华spent his last years with a cat, not writing, not womanizing
and尼采had no WeChat or FB to gather flatterers
the mental home being his home
someone is practicing night and
manufacturing dreams on a personal scale
佩索阿with no one living to claim

---

122 11/1/1983, Wuchang.
123 20/4/16, Madison, Wisconsin.

his living work B•S •约翰逊did become
famous after he filled his bathtub
with warm blood
when 'Black Beauty' was removed
there was no because, not even
explanation于斯曼did all right
乌勒贝克did better贝克特, too
even though the latter was full
of complaints of the bitterest kind
life suffered, for death's sake
普拉斯is fine, she had poetry that lives
怀特claimed he was a pessimist but he managed
to win the N and have asthmatic attacks
all the winners of the country A- but international minors
it takes years to restore one lost night
with all its raindrops in their original place
then some[124]

Post-truth

Something was shot
   and trashed
      嗓若寒磣
         材料：泥土、粘土、圆s
           b lack legs in b right scar let h eels
              舒服hygge soofoo
                 冒菜maocai冒充菜maochong cai
                 big oil big h air大油

["不能真实面对自己，就是对着镜子，也要弄一个虚幻的"云"。墓
地是为了自摸一样地弄出诗意。对不起，我是说目的。"][125]

---

124 29/5/16, HBL.
125 18/11/16, HBL.

Pretty

This is what they say about *you*:
好山好水好寂寞

As opposed to what they say about *us*:
好脏好乱好快活

Don't worry about not understanding it
I'll translate it for you:

Whereas *you* are
Pretty mountains, pretty waters but pretty lonely

We are
Pretty dirty pretty messy but pretty happy

Make sense?
Not them and us, but *you* and us[126]

道

道is not just road. It is a head rested on the foot or feet. Foot or feet in front of the head, leading the head towards the left, in the direction of the character, in the formation of the character. It is not just the way, either. A way has an 'ay' in it, like accosting someone when you are lost, unlike道, which has a head in it and a radical that indicates the act of walking. Head rested on the feet walking makes道. Easy enough a concept.

道is pronounced dao and in ancient times it was pronounced tao. Dao rhymes with a number of things: arrival, knives, islands, reversal, the last being quite

---

126 8/5/14, Sweebee Office.

real. If you look at the character, it indicates that the feet are leading the head, not the other way round. Think of a nation led by the feet. Dao also rhymes with leadership, theft, rice and dancing. Confused now but not enough yet? Then let's turn to tao, which rhymes with a number of other things: waves, escapes, peaches, and porcelain. It, in a sense, is right, as, after all, you use tao to initiate an escape, e.g. over waves much the way refugees seek freedom in countries most likely to put them in mental hospitals that are prisons and detention centres and that are also birth delivery wards. Perhaps better than dao, a knife, tao is a peach that reminds one of Tao Yuanming whose peach source remains something preferable to utopia whose reversal, or dao, is dystopia, for, as yet, there is no unpeach source invented.

道is enough for all the ways roads paths routes pavements groves avenues streets circulars cul-de-sacs for, as Mao put it decades ago when commenting on the Americans, those who have the dao have much help and those who lose the dao have little help. Nor is dao the 'process' Pound likes to refer and prefer to. For in an earthquake it is severed or cut or completely swallowed up. That's dao, too, that of the earth because people today have exhausted their dao, giving it away to the earth to exercise its own dao, or to the wheels or wings that tend to break or derail.

Pull

She's pulling you down
despite your resistance
her eyes pulling your eyes
out
you got bigger
in spite yourself
she wanted to be made shufu
and in making herself shufu
you were shufu, too
... [127]

---

[127] 11/10/16, HBL.

庞德说

脸书上有人晒了一封
庞德早年写的英文信
奉劝一位
东西写得不好的女士说：

Never ornament
Never writer a line
That you think
Is pretty or picturesque

随译成中文便是：
绝对不要修饰
绝对不要写一行你自以为
漂亮或风光的诗[128]

皮

《皮绊》一诗翻译讲完时
老诗问了一个问题：
"皮绊"究竟如何译？
是译成"piban"
还是别的什么
大多学生语塞
老诗便举例问：
"皮蛋"如何译？
"皮条客"呢？
"皮笑肉不笑"呢？
学生都笑了
还是说不出
老诗于是说，其实有一个很简单的方式

---

128 27/2/14, Kingsbury.

就是直接进入
皮蛋就是skin eggs
皮笑肉不笑就是
比如，他指着一个冲他笑的男生说：
His skin smiles but his flesh doesn't
总比你，他指着一个女生说
的那个"fake smile"要生动得多
要知道，中文这么丰富形象诗意的语言
英文哪有？
只有靠你们将来
直接输送过去
增加莎士比亚没有的
活气
然后，他又冲着那个很感兴趣的女生说：
至于拉皮条
不就是pull skin strip
当然，他做了一个拉手风琴的动作，说：
stretch skin strip
甚至不妨the一下，成为这样：
to stretch the skin strip
最后他收官，对"皮绊"的标题
下了结论：
如此如此，这般这般

请注意，没上这课的学生
要知后事，必得上课
才行
否则不公布
下文[129]

---

129 27/9/16, HBL.

鱼fish渔

魚、、、、、、、、、、、、、、、、、、、

fiiiiiiiiiiiiiiiiiiiiiiiiiiiiiiiiiiiiiiiiiiiiiiiiiiiiiiiiiiiiiiiiiish

渔、、、、、、、、、、、、、、、、、

情侣进行时

英语有人姓Love
汉语也有，姓艾
发音是一样的

英语有人姓Britain
汉语也有，但不姓
而叫"中国"，如盛中国

英语有人姓England
汉语也有，但不姓
而叫"英文"，如蔡英文

英语还有些姓
是匪夷所思、匪夷所诗的
仅举一例

昨夜有人发来电子邮件
我当即删去
但对落款人的姓名却稍有留意

该人姓Lovering
那是Lover（情侣）的进行时
意即lover, lover, lovering

如若译成中文

可能译成"拉夫林"
多难听的名字!

远不如
情侣进行时
来得好听

问：请问你贵姓？
答：哦，免贵姓
情侣进行时[130]

起舞

.
深冬转年的时候，桂花还在开，凑到鼻尖下，不香

..
什么地方的打桩机，把星期天的鸟都打得不吱声了

...
一个人，一碗稀饭，一碟咸菜，陪着一张一张一张桌子，吃饭

.....
我以为那是匹马，飘飞的黄发，再看像女的，再看还是马，雌马

....
已经很久不做爱了，不知道还会不会做，不知道找谁做

....
想起一个诗人，觉得：真不如从来都没见过的好

....
That's the life he prefers, known to all, known only, to himself

───────────
130 8/9/15, Kingsbury.

....
"你这叫只知其一，不知其二"。Must write this into the novel

....
Except that I might forget it。一天，又将在烟烧中燃尽

....
"我觉得还是一个人过好，自由自在极了。以后我们就这样分开过好吗？"

....
这是他们的节日，这里人不管，也要过，政府不让过

....
那些树，深棕色了，黑色的树干，鸟继续唱同样的调调也不厌倦

....
对每个人都说：Have a great Christmas and New Year!其实是抄过的。微信嘛

....
是得设立一个国际剽窃日了，让剽窃成性的学生大剽一整天至少

....
总觉得那人狡猾，又不知道怎么说，就发明了一词：jaw猾

....
今日作业标题：《潮湿》或《潮润》

....
拉空了的感觉，远比吃饱了好。射空也是如此

....
他妈的打桩机，在25号嚎

....
译成《嚎叫》绝对没有译成《嚎》好，原文就是一个字：Howl

150

....
他的东西表面裹着一层雅的糖衣，里面有脏货、脏力

....
身体里according to他，只有四样东西：blood, phlegm, filth, excreta

....
这四字来自塞林格女儿的回忆录：*Dream Catcher*, Scribner出版，2001, p. 417

....
'A disappointing Christmas meal mate. I hope you don't spend today on your own.'

....
He (PN) said above and I said here: 都去过tmd什么g8圣诞节去了

....
From email: 'Get ready for Christmas with this $500 Bunnings Gift Card!'

....
一大堆书要看。不看。一大堆事要做。不做。一大堆屎要拉。拉了

....
最可恨的是女人。最可爱的是女人。最可恶的依然还是女人

....
把自己归linche

....
我天天放假。天天工作。天天都烦。特别烦这一天，好像来了月圣经

....
"你儿子是该成亲了。要是我们这儿早就成亲了。"

....
"你们看上去好像都很happy嘛，不像我们那个时代，人人都不happy"

....

"当然是头道贩子比二道贩子好嘛，如果翻译的话"

....

"千万别，我从来不在任何群内。我是离群索居者"

....

多么阴险的心啊，人，看上去很和颜悦色的嘛

....

"哈哈，你的传统思想，一验证，就露馅"

....

又来一个信教的，真让人收不了

....

"所以说嘛，一生下来都是死胎才好，全宇宙死个干干净净"

....

这个世界，所有的人都处于假死状态

....

当年理想者，而今安在哉

....

NYJ: 'I made the determination of entering the society'

....

ZQ: 'The publishing house witness the boru of the book'

....

不跟个b日的来往

....

TXR: 'Also you will bear my bad temper'

....
Anons: 'accept my apologize', 'keep health', 'I really did not give a shit to him'

....
Anons: 'I hided myself', 'the whole money', 'I backed to home'
....
Anons: 'Guss what?' 'My boss yelled me into the phone', 'My farther'

....
Anons: 'before I lossing them', 'I don't care the gender'

....
"'请为我们采撷一束朝露'"：又是这种矫情的货色，砸死它"

....
"'阳光有着金色的良心／风掠过原野的绿色眼睛'：滥得勒，恶心"

....
"不看了"[131]

人说

人说：凭什么你制定规则？凭什么要听你的？

"某某"has recalled a message

人说：女人的逻辑

人说：男人就要听女人的逻辑

"某某"has recalled a message

---

131 25/12/16, HBL.

人说：就像书里说的那样
女人说：我认为是对的，那就是对的
因为我认为是对的

人说：女人就是每月血流坏的

"某某"has recalled a message
人说：整一个雄枭
"某某"has recalled a message

人说：雌路不通

"某某"has recalled a message

人说：雄关漫道真如饕

"某某"has recalled a message

人说：雌人说梦

"某某"has recalled a message

人说：英雄不如英雌

人说：英痴，还是？

"某某"has recalled a message

人说：割掉你，看你还敢雄起？！

"某某"has recalled a message

人说：我是女人我怕谁！

无语

人说：我是女人我怕睡！

"某某"has recalled a message

人说：那你找"穿过中国去shui你的"那个呀！

"某某"has recalled a message[132]

Sad

诗歌已经不sad了
这是多么大的一个loss
现在的人貌似都很happy
把bullets压进
Cartridge一样的
胸膛
诗歌真不sad了吗？
那谁还要喝
这杯bitter酒呢？
不能sad的诗歌
就像没有臭气的
屎[133]

Sadness

口岸签证处
电梯口声音：请抓好扶手，注意脚下安全（不断重复）
Please hold the handrail n mind your steps[134]

---

132 31/10/16, HBL.
133 8/9/15, Kingsbury.
134 22/5/15, Pudong Airport.

Scissors

早上抓阄写诗
先抓了两个，其中一个是pen
放弃了，因为规矩是抓一
再抓的就是上面
你们看到的那个字
这且不去说它了
且说我昨天上英语写作课
用的就是这个方法
有的抓了A，有的抓了Q
还有的抓了Africa
和love
以及death或ugliness
以及——凡是你们想得出
或想不出的字、数字、字
母，除了字公
抓A的那个来了一首
她平生第一首
英文诗，说：

A comes before B
B comes before C
C comes before D
D comes before E
…
until Z comes before A
A, A, A
Even if I never get straight A's
I've got it now
The first A in my life

写love的那个男生
一上来就romantic了
什么Cupid之类

让我想起，从前有个女生
上台朗诵时的一首诗结尾：
Love is shit
她说那是一个男生失恋后说的话
被她"偷"了过来
写Africa的那个，想了半天想出这几句：
I don't know anything about Africa
I've never been there
Now that it's in my hand
I recall having actually seen
Many Africans in my country
They are black, they are dark
And Chinese women love them

拿到ugliness的那个女生
也有惊人之语，她写道：
Summer is uglier than spring
But she's my best friend

写death的女孩也不示弱
她写道：
Winter is dead
Spring is dead
Summer is dead
And now, autumn is about to die

好了，该我写完这首题为"scissors"的诗了
一句话：
我所做的不过是把
现实和想象scissor了一下[135]

---

135 12/10/16, HBL.

Se

色即空
射即空

中国色
英语sex

X
An axe

That
Cuts[136]

Shi

每次大便之后
诗就会脱便而出
比如那首《大》
就是化便为神奇

有时边拉，诗
就会在大脑中凸起

总是这样，有多少屎
就会拉多少诗

比如今天写的《叫》
今天写的《至少》

后来我在那本书中
找到了出处

---

136 8/1/13, YSH.

他说：
"writing is like shitting"

他又说：
"reading the letters of Pushkin a little later

I found he said exactly
the same thing"[137]

他有没有意识到
Pushkin（普希金）的名字中

有个"push"，在英文中是"推"
在汉语中相当于"拉"?

我们的诗和我们的屎
本来都是同根生

拉出去的冲掉了
拉出来的留下了

李白也好、杜甫也好
欧阳修也好、莎士比亚也好

你读到的他们
不都是拉出来的shi? [138]

Shi坛

结dung营shit[139]

---

137 Patrick White, *Patrick White Speaks*. Primavera Press, Sydney: 1989, p. 22.
138 27/5/16, HBL.
139 29/12/16, HBL.

Solid State Drive

时间／在这儿／沉淀／成天
我对时间／也不太那么／care 了
don't worry about it

*　　　*　　　*

the loins of time
            still throbbing
            hard, years after

*　　　*　　　*

而我只希望
我自己身体的
            国家灭亡

*　　　*　　　*

a throat singing: *I'm never going to sleep*
            alone again
一具有意思的身／体

*　　　*　　　*

the man of yesterday recorded:
            so suddenly I'm in love
            with a stranger

*　　　*　　　*

will you take it back please
            who wants the most advanced technology
            一百年之前的

160

and that c—t
remains as fresh
as a foto graph[140]

势力眼

The powerful and profitable eye
An eye focused on the powerful
And profitable side of things
Or of beings

The eye of a person
That avoids seeing
What is not
Powerful and profitable[141]

时间

把时间放下来
忘掉时间、拿掉时间
擦、擦、擦净时间
把时间砸成碎片、擦成碎片
一片片地擦时间、擦时空间、时阴间
在时间隙里生活
进入时无间
把时间hold still
dream in时间in时人间in时心间
time times time约等于timelss约等于tmeless约等于tmlss
把时间消失在鸟嘴
消失小时消逝小诗小食消食小石销蚀消释
hours h ours hour s h our s xiaoshi

---

140 12/2/17, Kingsbury.
141 8/11/12, Hongqiao Airport.

s间的停尸间时jian的挺尸jian时jian的停驶jian
一片片地擦shi间、擦shi空间、擦时停尸间

timeless间timless阴间timeless心间[142]

时间观念

应该是1992年2月的一天
她跟孩子还没来澳洲join我之前
我从Southern Road骑车
去Kingsbury的Cash Street跟Geoff
为看房见面
我抵达时，一分不早，一分不晚
Geoff，一个高个子英国男人
对我说了一句，2016年7月2日星期六的2.34pm
我还记得：You are a man after my own heart
我当然不是一个man after his own heart
我甚至都不是一个man after my own heart
我知道，他指的是时间方面
我是这样一个after his own heart的人
过了二十四年，在松江、在SUIBE
我11点吃中饭，11.11分去办公室
在那儿等头天约好，今天11.30分
来还书的学生
我在办公室，把所有
乱六七糟的东西：可以再度在澳大利亚
使用的已经用过的牛皮信封
已经看过本不想带走但最后还是决定带走的朋友
送我的诗集和书，因为某本的空页上
还写着我的诗迹
以及我用自己劳动人民的手
制作的一本本大大小小的ecological《生命之书》

---

142 24/2/17, Kingsbury.

这些做完之后，装了满满四袋
学生还没来
直到我离开的11.35分还是没来
我火了，说了"恶心之极"这样的话
总共说了两次
我背着一个袋子，拎着三个袋子
陪我自己，走回宾馆房间
我没有想到，我教的研究生居然
如此没有时间观念
我想起小时候母亲骂我时常说的一句话：
是牛，穿鼻子也教醒了！
Geoff是1992年
而在2016年的中国
一切都没有改变
难怪Gig不来
难怪Steve不来
难怪Michael不来
难怪—我该请自己走了
恕我不再有言[143]

死

人在未死之前
差不多就已经死了
或者快死了

就像刚才
给朋友打电话那样
寒暄过后，居然无话可说

也像刚才
看过的一个老友
或者说发小的文字

---

143 2/7/16, HBL.

他在其中说
父亲临终前
他去看他

父亲只看他一眼
就再也没说话
直到生命体征成一条直线

我产生了一部长篇的开头
是这样写的：
I've made an entry today in my diary

That I shall die on such and such a date
Best of all, on the date of my birth, in one year's time
And, prior to that date coming, I shall

Begin on this novel by telling
A simple tale of my life
Hiding nothing, transparent to the degree

Of a night....
我想象的小说
到此也已结束

但我不在乎死
哪怕现在她与我牵手
我也会非常happy，非常非常happy[144]

睡

把人
打伤
致残

把人
梦死在
床上

把人
像那部
长篇写的：

The novelist
died
in one of his dreams when his wife came out of it and called…

把人
打得
诗花缭乱

起来
老婆喊
起来！ [145]

睡

只要一睡着，就会走远，走到天的反面
手指头在衣角，抱，进入深处，无底
那时是反的，如果头朝下，生命的产生即如此
走了的还在，在者不存，有人，在哼
都想快啊，一岁已熟，纸质的天空，空天的纸
在洞里遨游，通过洞而呼吸，鱼贯
Reardon和Biffen，还有Crystal，以及
Des Esseintes，人然
花心的癌症[146]

---

145 12/9/15, Kingsbury.
146 25/7/15, Kingsbury.

The later arrival

That day, I began my morning creative writing class
With a poem, *jiaru wo you yi gan qiang*, from Australia
And I read, in Chinese, *wo yao shasi...de nanren*
wo yao shasi...de nanren
wo yao shasi...de nanren
When the door was squeezed open and the head of
A habitual late arriver
Popped in
Immediately, I switched
Into English as my finger was pointed his way:

If I had a gun I'd kill the man
Who came so late
And I'd kill the man
Who had missed out on the first part
Of this great poem
And I'd kill the man---my reading
Interrupted by a loud laughter
Of my 40-odd female students before I was able to resume
My Chinese reading of the rest
Of the poem as the man
Found his seat, quietly and perplexed
In the crowded room
The good news, though, is
One girl was so interested in the poem
That she emailed for a copy and wanted to know who
The poet was[147]

---

147 25/5/14, YSH.

The Philosopher/Historian/Linguist Said

The Chinese have this great way of creating words that make sense
Good is not a woman with a child
Good is a woman with a man
The woman on the left and the man, on the right
And, according to the *I-Ching*, or *The Book of Change*
The left is meant to be superior
Hence the superior woman on the left to her man on the right
Represents the word hao好or good

Take poetry, too
It is generally thought that it consists of two words
Speech on the left and a temple on the right
Giving the impression that poetry is about speaking
By the side of a temple
When in fact the word si寺does not stand for the temple
It stands for the law, the law court, the government
In ancient times, exactly the same way ci词
The new kind of poetry that appeared in the Song Dynasty works
For poetry is not something that you write to please yourself
Or even to please the public, the enlarged image of your self
It is a tool used to govern the people
The ordinary and the lowly educated, with no training in poetry
A tool used to carry dao道the way, as the saying goes:
Literature exists for the purpose of carrying the way
So does poetry, if that makes sense[148]

The quote

我已经死了
死了一百次
一千次

---

148 22/12/12, Sanya U.

一万次
我已经死了一亿次
我和周围所有的人毫无区别
整天为了前途未卜的目标而忙碌
完全忽视了生活中最本质
最珍贵的精髓

of course you don't understand, he says
so let me give it a pinyin
just for the sound:

wo yijing sile
sile yibaici
yiqianci
yiwanci
wo yijing sile yiyici
wo he zhouwei suoyou de ren haowu qubie
zhengtian weile qiantu weibu de mubiao er manglu
wanquan hushi le shenghuo zhong zui benzhi
zui zhenggui de jingsui

and, of course, he says
I know you remain the one
who doesn't know, so let me attempt a translation, for you:

I've died
Died a hundred times
Died a thousand times
Died ten thousand times
I have died one hundred million times
I'm no different from people around me
Busy all day with objectives with an unpredictable future
Completely ignoring the most essential, the most treasured
Marrow of life

Just a quote, the man says, put on the backcover
Of a republished novel in 2016, written in Mandarin, by 欧阳昱
Hand-written 27 years ago and self-published 17 years ago[149]

Them and Us

我们兴风，他们作浪 (making waves)
我们自擂，他们自吹 (blowing one's own trumpet)
我们不说，他们说不 (saying no)
我们三思，他们二思 (thinking twice)
我们活口，他们养家 (raise a family)
我们大同，他们小异 (more of the same)
我们说爱，他们谈情 (talk about love)
我们无天，他们无法 (lawless)
我们远航，他们扬帆 (set sail)
我们动工，他们破土 (break ground)
我们地设，他们天造 (make in heaven)
我们咬牙，他们切齿 (gnash one's teeth)
我们扬镳，他们分道 (parting ways with)
我们人山，他们人海 (a sea of people)
我们火热，他们水深 (in deep waters)
我们共济，他们同舟 (in the same boat)
我们忍气，他们吞声 (swallowing an insult)
我们吐气，他们扬眉 (lifted brow)
我们养晦，他们韬光 (hiding the light)
我们虎咽，他们狼吞 (wolfing down)
我们一心，他们一意 (single-minded)
我们铜墙，他们铁壁 (bastion of iron)
我们在，他们不在 (absent)
他们在 (present)，我们不在[150]

---

149 25/3/16, HBL.
150 10/4/16, HBL.

them

让研究生翻译一篇
墨尔本赛马节的报纸文章
第一句上来就是：
"You could hear them before you could see them."
　［原文链接见此：http://www.theage.com.au/victoria/melbourne-cup-
2016-the-riches-that-lay-beneath-the-rubbish-when-punters-leave-20161101-
gsfqox.html］
一个研究生在黑板上这么译道：
"在没有看到它们之前就能它们的声音。"
显然漏掉了"听到"
年轻人忘性大，也是常有的事
但简单的文字
能够这么简单地译？
教授提醒：想想《红楼梦》里怎么说的
这一下，大家来劲了
立刻有人说：未见其人，先闻其声
教授提醒说：可这个"them"指的不是"人"
而是seagulls（海鸥）啊
于是有人说：那老师
能不能译成：
未见海鸥，先闻其声呢？
另一个学生说：
开篇第一句，并未提海鸥
而是吊胃口，只说是"them"
这就有意思了，教授说
汉语一向傲娇，总以为自己的那个ta
不写出来就听不明白
不知道是他、她，还是它
人家英文虽然有he、she和it
但人家的"them"
就很模糊，看不出是
他们、她们，还是它们
这就是为何开篇第一句

170

就玩了一个"them"
下课走在回"家"的路上
教授想：无论是那个
"未见海鸥，先闻其声"
或"未见它们，先闻其声"
以及自己建议的"未见其鸥，先闻其声"
似乎都不太合适
想到这里，他低低地，喊了一声
说：有了
他的译文，暂不公示
请"them"继续译吧

[后注：他的译文是："未见其影，先闻其声"。] [151]

Things

There are things that must be said
It's not just for 'fun', as you put it

Kafka is a friend in that I knew
His other acquaintances could have said the same

Pessoa, too, who had not made a buck
From the sales of his poems that appeal, post-life

Like Van Gogh, whose ear was so angry
It didn't survive his billion-dollar paintings

Dickinson as well, who must have thought
Oh, my secret thoughts are mine, not for the likes of You

There are lots more, like them, like me
Wishing for a life, they and I, don't deserve

---

151 11/11/16, HBL.

If it were merely fit for a living pig
As they book their death long before they leave

Whether others give a life, papery or digital
It's none of my bu诗ness[152]

Balanced

All hell breaks loose
All heaven breaks tight

Where there is a will there is a way
Where there is a way there is a wheel

If Lee Hsien Loong has a short tempter according to the holy Goh
I prefer to have a long temper

I wrote something in a Chinese poem that my professor liked
It's basically like saying people begin with offering their hand

And end with offering their foot
And so many people are now born with an itching palm

Will that not turn into an aching one sometimes?
Fit like a glove and fit like a love, too

And what was this that was on the tip of my tongue a second ago?
Oh, I see, it was "mum benefit" that was actually "maximum benefit"with a -turn

So, let's continue: a little pot is soon hot
A hot pot is soon big

If you marry a fortune

---

152 4/12/13, RSH.

You can also marry a misfortune

Ah, I now hear the devil's tattoo
And I hear the god's tattoo, too

You put in your two cents worth
And I'll put in my one cent worth

All is well that ends well
Well is all that ends all

Too late

脸，女人就是一张脸
女人知道：只要把脸弄得perfect
Everything will be all right
等到一切都成了之后
Everything will be too late
女人的名字就叫：Too Late
涂•雷特女士[153]

Two宰场

磨刀whore whore

天

loud天
word天
chant天
chin天
yin天

---

153 17/2/17, Kingsbury.

man天
sin天
ban天
hung天
leo天
the天
gene天
loo天
urine天
tongue天[154]

苔丝：一个细节

当时，*Graphic*杂志的编辑
来信说
Angel Clare把苔丝
和另外三个挤奶姑娘
抱在怀里
从洪水淹没的小巷子里
抱过去
很不合适
因为这个杂志
的读者
都是有家室的人
他建议
最好把那个细节改一下
让男的用独轮
手推车
把女的推过去
这样才比较
Decorous and suitable
（端庄得体而且恰如其分）
哈代说：

---

154 18/12/16, HBL.

174

This was accordingly done
意思就是说:
就按他意思改了 [155]

Value

A fighter plane
Normally costs about 1 to 3 million in US dollars

A绿头鸭 (Lütou ya)
Or green-headed duck

Costs about 70 yuan in RMB
Equivalent to about 15 Aussie dollars

Towards the end of 2015
A Chinese green-headed duck, in an ecologically rich area

Turned herself into a suicide bomber
By flying into a Chinese fighter plane

Causing it to crash, into her family pond
Warranting the news of the year

A green-headed duck
As green as a poem [156]

---

155 参见 *The Life of Thomas Hardy: 1840-1928* by Thomas and Florence Hardy. Wordsworth Editions, 2007, p. 247, written 6/9/14, Kingsbury.
156 29/12/15, HBL.

WA

WA的云好大
WA的星星好亮
WA的风很响

WA是一个
从未想到要去的地方
WA的时间是异故乡 [157]

WeChat

Welcome back, you trillions and more
Dead for hundreds of thousands
Of years
To this Chinese
Invention enabling them to exhibit
Their daily shit
Via a toy mobile
Phony
Where you witness the new
Century unfold under your collective nose
By a bunch
Of weixin politicians weixin
Professors weixin philosophers weixin
Poets weixin photographers weixin collectors
Of wisdom weixin celebrators of all kinds of festive
Occasions weixin players of life weixin wasters and wastrels
Of time if you leave
Instantly I won't blame you and I applaud
Your decision, too
For who wants to live

---

157 22/8/15, Kingsbury.

A life as trashy as weixin
Invented by a people whose only desire for life
Is expect the next click
On喜欢？ [158]

Wind Bones

"他是一个很有风骨的人"
Bones in the wind
Or wind in the bones
But他不是他
也不是他、也不是他、也不是他
他走了，不打招呼，就走了，gone
With the bones
And the风
仅仅只是一个眼风，a wind of eye
an eye wind
such a man of wind bones
他的bones里有着
无法为当代吸收的wind[159]

Word天

Frieday
见needle插缝
哈哈heart
to豪
word爹
厉high了word妹
懵b
二b
可以这很p股

158 11/5/14, YSH.
159 3/6/16, HBL.

大家shanghai
神horse都是浮cloud
一word马
who说8道
what梗
实时热dot
ta奶的[160]

万念

其实想想，万念俱ashes，也是一种，很好的，感觉
像那时那样，ten thousand念俱灰一下，什么都不想做
一眼望穿，未来，不都是，要死的吗，一根根，枯骨，而已
万ideas俱灰，像此时这样，决定，又未完全决定，是否
今天什么事，都不干，以后是否，完全与谁、谁谁、谁谁谁
不来往，是否根本，不再，活，下去
万念all灰，What a chengyu!，只能这么，玩下去了
再睁开眼时，脑体不是倒挂，而是上载了
mind uploading, into a completely, new, fu, ture
looking back, on, the, animals, now, living[161]

无语

你把一生最好的二十二年
抛在了一个怎么也变不成故乡的异乡
You've squandered the best 22 years of your life
In an alien village that refuses to be turned into a native one

你作出最大的努力
却收获风和最小的果实
You've made the maximum effort
In reaping the wind and the smallest fruit

---

160 5/11/16, HBL.
161 25/2/17, Kingsbury.

178

你在一年最寒冷的时候买了一台最大供热力为1200瓦的加热器
你买了皮蛋你买了铅你买了生姜你还买了黄瓜

You in the coldest time have bought a heater with a maximum 1200 kw capacity
You've bought skin eggs lead raw ginger and yellow melons

你沿着扶梯上行时并不伤心地感到伤心
你想回到这个早已不属于你国家的国家养老送终也不是不可以

You go upwards in the escalator feeling broken-hearted not feeling so
You think it possibly not impossible you keep till death in this country long not yours

你只觉得再怎么努力那个异乡也不会承认
你终究认输就像他们终究也会认输一样

You don't think you'll ever reach recognition in that village however hard you try
You'll eventually accept failure the same way they'll accept it, too

你无语你想到那个国家就无语
你沉默地走回租屋顺便把日暮最美的丑景摄入眼睛相机

You wordless and wordless at the thought of that country
You walk back to your room silently taking in your eyes the most beautiful ugly scene[162]

木又寸

木tree又寸
木又tree寸
t木r又e寸e
木又tree寸
木tree又寸
木又寸

---

162 1/1/13, YSH.

问题

你哪来的那么多精力
写那么多东西? 出那么多书?

How did you manage to be so productive, so prolific
Did you never sleep?

他对第一个问题
的回答很简单:

没人可射的精
成就了你问的那个"精力"

他对第二个问题的回答
就不那么简单了

只能也用
英文回答:

I slept a lot
I had so many forgotten dreams

They are my failures
Which is why[163]

声音

"夜里曾被, 雨声惊醒"

"早晨雨中, 有人扫地"

"你不能等雨, 停了再扫吗? "

---

163 22/12/15, HBL.

"不回复，也无所谓"

"下了这么多的雨，也没人给它颁奖"

"每次提到得奖时，她总要重复两次"

"活不下去的时候，活下去"

"出现了一种，多余的声音"

"什么都不像"

"In a post-reader age, one writes, not to get published"

"He's persecuting you and not aware of it"

"自私的表现就是：只看人评他，绝不评他人"

"Becoming disengaged and that is poetry"

心 or Heart

Is heart meant to hear
or an organ of art

why is it matched with
心，with three drops of water

When 心 lies like this
horizontally, it is over-determined

but if it stands vertical
like this 忄, a lean-to with 青

green and spring
something more than love or愛

see that there is心inside it
and that it lies horizontal

so determined
but when 忄 is left and青is right

like this：情
minus one drop of water
it stands straight
like spring

not determined
but more determined

because it is ever
green

it happens when one grows past
a certain age[164]

心意

"也是一点心意"
她说

"知道心意英文怎么说吗？"
他问

"Heart？"
她抬起头来，望住我的眼睛

---

164 5/6/16, HBL.

"No, "我说
避开她的眼睛

"Heartmind"
我说，"Or，a hearted mind"

"一点心意"
她说，轻声地

"恩"
我说[165]

细胞

日子像癌细胞一样扩散
few worth recalling without rancor
雨又冷透了脊梁
smoke and ashes, drips and light, a she ditched
那鸟展翅的样子，对人类无比的恐惧
morning is growing, like cancer
厌倦了人世，在想：从哪儿可以更成功地起跳
four feet, wearily drawing to a close
所有的自，都成仁了，不，去掉单人旁，成二
the one must have died a long time ago, forsooth[166]

西方

你觉得里面有人
就把门推开
里面又是一扇门
你又推开
那个你觉得可能存在的人

165 7/10/16, HBL.
166 3/6/16, HBL.

你却看不见
返回身来
他也不在后面
这时，你想写的那首诗《西方》
出现了：where the sun sets
with much blood
and people still keep going
regardlessly[167]

谐音

2013.1.4: 爱您一生一世
What a chilling reminder of the lies told in exactly the same terms

Now, how about 2013.1.3
爱您妖三窃三

And what about 2013.1.2
爱您妖三要日

And also 2013.1.1
爱您妖三要要

All holy crap
And more, tomorrow: 2013.1.5

爱您妖三要我or妖我
And the day after: 2013.1.6

爱您妖三要溜or要流
And one more, to hit the road with

---

167 21/10/13, YSH.

爱您妖三要吃....
I haven't got all day, though[168]

Yeu

英文的"I"
是我
与汉语的"爱"同音

越南文的"Yeu"
是"爱"
与英文的"you"同音

这么说来，"I love you"
把中英越南文揉在一起
就是"爱、爱、爱"的意思

我则更喜欢
"Yeu Yeu Yeu"：
你你你，爱爱爱[169]

严峻

爱情很严峻啊
爱情的situation很严峻啊
谁跟谁都不来往了
Who跟who啊
Who该对who先主动啊
谁欠who啊
Who欠谁啊
爱情的situation很serious啊

---

168 4/1/13, YSH.
169 3/4/16, HBL.

大家都不来往也ok
让来往的人跟来往的人laiwang吧[170]

双诗

一整棵光秃秃的树
The whole tree without a leaf, a single leaf

、

沿河都是蓬蒿，或许是茅草
A dead tree, long skinned, long itself, lying

、

闪光变黄了，亮得不敢直视，很丑的，到处都是
The sky is bluer, against the clouds whiter, just one or two, or three

、

从这条路下去，左拐，穿过无用的深草，都是枯灰的
From above this man is seen walking, alone, photographing on his phone

、

如果实验诗人来，大约是要把这一切，连同他自己都烧掉吧
And inscribing a mere word or two, on the dead body of a tree

、

这里的一切都不卖，都卖不动，因此无眼搜寻，无足践踏
Days after, they'll be there, remaining bilingual, and ignored

170 2/10/16, HBL.

不可能孤独，在这儿，天空是最好的朋友，还有始终守候的树
Light and shadows, bright and ark, I meant dark, but it's equally right, behind a b

、

看不见水的色，看不见色的水，过河的地方，低了下去，听见水响
And she said: I've got pregnant, even though I've not touched a man for a century

、

绿的黄的枯黄的黑的焦黑的阳黄的叶青的草鲜的天白的云香的
One doesn't need to write one just moves his feet one looks around one thinks little

、

那边墙上的树，影得很子，黑色斑块中，透着空明，横的，斜的
Put the word, in the eye of a bird, a chirping bird, on its flight

月下行

No one will remember this evening. Not cold. Quiet. Luoye caca zai jiaoxia zuoxiang. One remembers something. A woman. One says to oneself, in loud thoughts, if you will: it's not entirely memorable if one wants to be honest with oneself. Jishi zai dangshi, nazhong ganjue, cong chengdu shang lai jiang, ye zhineng shuo pingdan eryi. Dangran not as good as the other one. Oh, what a she! She ba ni laxiashui. She ba ni daishangchuang. She, zoubian tianya genzhe ni. She, you name yidian scary. 她与time长成一体。

我不是Charles Dickens，但我记得，他被人提起经常chuanguo城市，观察人，观察他们的xiangmao，样貌，我也同样穿过城市，but I felt uncomfortable because my bladder was filling up, my bad bladder。我环顾四周，又是一个湖，湖边的树，没有隐身的可能。对面走来的，都是女的，看不清面目。像学生。像学生？长什么样？穿什么衣服？漂亮还是丑？Who the fuck knows? And who gives a fuck if they are pretty or not? None of my business。但这个男人擦身而过时，看了我一眼，那种眼神，仿佛在探究。

187

在问：你也？你是不是？如果我说：yes, please，我们会回到Cavafy当年的亚历山大港吗？我们会重新进入那首流血的诗吗？

I saw that café again, yes, that's right, that's the right place. It's now called SoSo. It didn't seem the one Tom and I were at last time he was here. But it looked like it, quite empty, with one girl at the bar table. She looked at me, through the glass. And I looked back at her, not a student, not the one we met last time. Like last time, I went to the lift and stopped to look at the names on the side. Nothing like last time. Only memories, of red lights and green, and prices offered.

Henxiang laniao. Zou huiqu. Guojie. Xiang zhaoge defang la, dan dengguang ba suoyou difang zhaode bushuang. Zhentamade bu shufu. You laidao natiao xiaojie, youkandao nage zhiya he zuyu de difang. Genzi hen chang. Chaochang. Or should I say super-high? Super-tall? But there's a cluster of people there. Oh, the pain of being gazed at by all eyes and having to choose one among many.

我想把這個男人帶回去，讓他重新體驗，雙手把高跟捏在手裡，像操縱器一樣挺進的滋味，從一個洞進入無數洞，把自己的精和力灑在極近的遠方。我想帶著他走遍寬廣的雌性國土，在防空洞中躲避世事的紛擾，讓發臭的鈔票說著肉話，拋一堆液體垃圾給裝飾的顏值。我想帶著這個人足浴，以足弓彈射慾望的綠唇。But zhege ren hanle, zhege ren buxing, zhege ren wangzhe limian, ta xiang, ta bugan, ta dui ziji shuo: yaoshi tangmu zai jiu haole, zheshi zuihao you liangren zai yiqi.

月亮，你又看着他从荒野穿过，一个孤零零的四足，与一个到跟前才看清一定是来自印度次大陆的脸的人相遇。他多想说：Hey, how you going?等他回过头，那人已经走远，一生的唯一一次月下机会，就这样永久地失落。Ah, poetry落。失落st。他买了一本书。他看见那个不起眼的母亲，在12月上旬和中旬之交的那个8点钟的晚上，坐在书店看书不回家，让女儿在她身边一遍遍地问：好看吗？好看吗？却一句也不睬她，管自看她可能一直要看到书店关门才不看的书。这不会是一个有着严重抑郁症的人吧？不会是一个离婚女人吧？外面，男男女女搂搂抱抱，在走廊并非专门为他们准备的长椅上，你的眼睛从他们身上溜过，却看见一张肥肥的雌脸。绝不可能了，一切美颜。

The moon.月亮。照着人在走的moonlight. Yueliang. Yue de liang.[171]

有人

Someone paradies
有人在天堂死了
He misses hell
他怀念地狱
The tree in paradise
天堂树
Has roots
根深
In hell
地固
The face of love
爱之脸
Is sinister
很狰狞[172]

野蛮

这雨就是很野蛮
也不管你喜不喜欢
它一个劲地down、down、down
所有停下的车
都披上雨皮
Rain skin is no racist
As it has no colour
更深入地进入孤

---

171 10/12/16, HBL.
172 17/1/14, Kingsbury.

和独
这种野蛮的雨
管你爱听不听
满耳灌的都是雨
声
湿透你的踵
那个等待中的人始终
不露face
她跟雨一样wild蛮[173]

雨 rainyu

Operated on by the rain, he turns into 雨
Wind in the 雨，touching the areas that are 湿
On the back of the lower legs, and the 脚尖
A decaying mind is a pain, less than 雨
One'd rather listen to the 音 of 雨
Its presence doesn't need to selfie its 重要
The drop, at its lightest, falls and the 风
Loves the way it 雨 s
It's rather 雨来疯
Over there, a heart de-cored
Inside an ageing 肉
体
fast person fast 雨[174]

Miss Takes Taken

Don't be 累 zy
Or 雷 zy

番人 ners never learn

---

173 3/6/16, HBL.
174 3/6/16, HBL.

they really are烦人ner

Some like to play skytrue
Which is, of course, not my菲vourites

Shakespeare sai: Chinese students doo two much
ho me work bcaus they want2 bcom confucious

If you做that
My you live in intriguing time

But I know瓦特that is:
Rather be a太平dog,　不做乱世woman

Yellow long gone
Memory still a赖夫

正能量

One often hears this on TV or reads it in the news
Here in this country as positive as the other country is negative
Full of负能量
They reject
They say no
They disapprove of anything and everything
Till they find themselves a disappearance here
I'm not going to explain
Even if you say please
If it is life here
It is death there
Even if the life here is filled with poison
And the life there seems永ternal

'You want to compete with me
in expe验mentation?

正负

看一个人是否有病，尤其是
看ta是否得了大病、重病
如爱博拉、爱滋病、爱恨病
那些以爱开头的病
就要检查ta
是否呈positive
　（那是正能量的正）
正如今晨昆士兰一名女医生
出现在报端
说：经爱博拉病检查
她呈negative
　（那是负能量的负）
她高兴得难以自拔
不能自己

一个有病的社会
经自检还发现
很positive（正）
还鼓励大家都positive
那就要小心又小心
正如一个人
只有被发现negative
才happy[175]

照猫画虎

A copy cat that copies
And turns
Itself into a tiger[176]

---

175 10/10/14, YSH.
176 10/11/12, Shantou U.

192

Ing

I'm wenting home in the rain, ho-me, that is
Even when someone is talkeding about G. M. Pumpkins
And I am wroting poultry, if you lyke, so to spoke
You are thoughting you啊supre-me
The rain is still in the ref-rain, the rest-rain, oh, the g-rain
Licking things woo-den, wooeden, wooedingden
So y don't we play with Ou Li Po
Po Li Ou or simplysimple: Po Li O
I am shatting
O, r u?
The sky, not to b outdung
Indeed, not to be outdunged
Is诗ting, too

籽

人活着就是用来分开的
谁都不是粘合体
carving myself
with a most abstract birth
day gift
诗陷囵圄
早晨地上的鱼肝油
看似石
榴籽
亮亮的里面
一颗
籽
丑即美[177]

---

177 27/10/16, HBL.

终yu出shi了

他said他没法写那个布勒伯
噢，卖糕的
she又said她绝对不join回来
啊，埋膏的
这些天的某一个half-night三点
a certain店为他wash了bowels
借他人为他买的slip
现在想起来都bellyache
人又come而gone
我impossible加以stop
什么world
真是one tar hoo too
彻底won dan le
but this is a国家where people
you die me alive[178]

转述

一人说：He wants to kill all the people in the world
因女人嫌他丑嫌他穷不爱他
还因另一女跟他好时同时跟其他另外3男有染

一人说：When kissed for the first time, the girl says: Can I have more？
因此她觉得那女孩特棒
值得她学习效仿

一人说：Because I did badly, the teacher always sat me in the worst seat
她英文依然没有太大起色
但她教授却从未这么做过

一人说：When her husband died, Grandma did not shed a single tear

---

178 19/10/16, HBL.

他问为什么，得到的回答是：
并没有觉得他已经走了

一人说：Divorced, a woman becomes more powerful
一人说：She had a girlfriend who kissed her but she decided to part company
一人说：The husband got angry and hit his wife on the head with a brick

这些、这些、这些
都是我批改完创意写作课手制书后
从记忆中所做的转述[179]

翻译

'Mother's stomach bellied out like a sail'
"母亲的胃像船帆一样鼓起"

'never, after she'd had me did she allow another man to enter her'
"她也从未问过我，是否允许别的男人进入她的身体"

'She new she had probably made a mistake with her contraceptive, but went ahead,
                                                                alive to the risk'
"她知道她可能在避孕上犯了个错，但继续生活，便意识到了这个危机"

'The did it quickly, against a wall. She had known him years before; it hadn't been
                                                    a grand passion, more like a baby grand'
"他们在一堵墙上很快做完。妈妈认识他很多年了，这次做爱不像是激情
                                    澎湃而做，而是为了孕育一个伟大的生命"

'The did it quickly, against a wall. She had known him years before; it hadn't been
                                                    a grand passion, more like a baby grand'
"他们靠墙，很快就干完了。母亲已认识他多年，以前激情不大，更像是
                                                            小激情"

---

179 23/6/16, HBL.

'I think she half wanted to have a baby'
"我觉得她并不想要孩子"

'they'd been having inter-course regularly and often, including one before breakfast that day, and one after Boyce---that is, after lunch'
"他们和往常一样经常做爱，包括那天早饭之前。在午饭之后，母亲和鲍伊斯做完爱之后，又和另外一个人做了一次"

'It only took a minute or two, nine months before I was born'
"几个月后，我的出生只花了一到两分钟"

'but my mother said he seemed uneasy, on edge, playing his role as if he expected someone to trump it'
"但我母亲说对方看起来很急躁，很疯狂，整个过程就好像有人会把他比下去一样"

'He came quickly, and released her'
"他来得很快，释放了母亲"

'Boyce folded the handkerchief with the leaked semen…went…into the cold air and stood looking down the snow-covered valley'
"布易斯沾有漏出精液的手帕折起来，放在口袋里，……进入寒冷的空气中，放在那里看着白雪覆盖的山谷"

[Note: The lines in English are taken from *A Woman of the Future* by David Ireland, published by Text in 2014. And the Chinese lines below each English line are quoted from translation exam papers by my MTI postgraduate students near the end of 2017]

At the end

of the day
what
we have
wanted has been
given us
out of the day
even though we knew little
about the day then
the first up
or not
oops after oops
temper after temper
things planned happened
as things had been
things unplanned happened
as things unplanned did
someone died again
someone was writing about death
totally unrelated
life writing, they call it
or 'foreword', actually a review
no one was pleased, it seems
and nothing to believe in
a phubber, phubbers
hooked to a hand-held
thinger
another waste
land laid
bare in the brains
anything to look
forward to
a night of death
alive with meng

奥登

上的那个破课本
关于奥登的
小传，居然不提那事

我让学生看这个链接：
https://en.wikipedia.org/wiki/W._H._Auden
慢慢下拉、慢慢下拉、慢慢下拉

拉到这一段，停下来了：
From around 1927 to 1939
Auden and Isherwood maintained a lasting

but intermittent sexual friendship
while both had briefer but more intense
relations with other men.

In 1939 Auden fell in love
with Chester Kallman
and regarded their relation as a marriage

我没点名让学生翻译此段
而是写此诗时，为读者计
把它翻译出来：

"从大约1927年到1939年
奥登和衣修伍德保持了一段持久
但时断时续的性友关系

同时还与其他男子发生了
更简短、也更强烈的关系
1939年，奥登爱上了

切斯特•卡尔曼
并视他们之间的关系为婚姻”
我诗完了[180]

Can

看山是mountains
看水是waters

看山不是mountains
看水不是waters

看mountains仍是山
看waters仍是水

看mountains是水
看waters是山

看山不是waters
看水不是mountains

看山是山waters
看水是水mountains

Seeing山as waters that are not山
Seeing水as mountains that are not水

看山that are watered mountains
看水that are mountainous waters

看that is mountains
看that is waters

---

180 1/4/17, HBL.

199

看that is seeing
看that is looking

kan that is watching
kan that is peering

不看山是mountains
不看水是waters

不看山不是mountains
不看水不是waters

不看mountains仍是山
不看waters仍是水[181]

Confinement

这个字，有关禁闭的意思
among other things
一见这词，我就想起
曾被我写进诗中的一件
说小不小，说大不大
的事
那诗收进了《永居异乡》一书
是写那个婴儿的
好像叫《十天》吧
跟那个Australian nurse一起在电梯里时
她提到了中国的坐月子这种做法
称其为"cultural confinement"
我未辩解——我又不是女人
但我听了不舒服
什么！"文化禁闭"？
我是否当场纠正她

记忆不得而知
但从 *A History of the Wife* 中
我终于得知 "lying-in" 这个字
原来，我们对西方妇女的认识
是不准确、也很偏见的
她们是人、是女人
她们生了孩子后
也要坐月子的
哦，不，那叫 "睡月子"
因为是 "lying-in"
而不是 "sitting-in"
其长度不是太长（两个月）
就是太短（两个星期）
也就是说
她们也有她们的 "cultural confinement"
What an alliteration!
她们也是女人、也是人
根本就是常识
其实，她们、他们把性
进行到底
最后 confined
在子宫里的
不是鱼
也不是雨
还是一个 baby 而已[182]

反了

每次讲课，老师总要
挑一些片语来当堂考考
那些英文系的学生
他们学英文的时候忘了中文

---

182 30/4/17, HBL.

学中文的时候忘了英文
比如有句片语是这么说的：
he knew it like the back of his hand
有个被点起来的学生说：
他知道得易如反掌
还有个说：他对此事了如指掌
老实说：都不是
如果直译，那就是
"他对此事的了解，就像了解他自己的手背"
换言之，他"了如手背"
正好与中文相反
你了如指掌、他了如手背
你还多了一个指头的"指"

跟着，老师又举一例
来自奥登"The More Loving One"这首诗
里面有两句是这么说的：
"Looking up at the stars, I know quite well
That, for all they care, I can go to hell"
（参见：https://www.poets.org/poetsorg/poem/more-loving-one）
老师问：谁能告诉我
"for all they care, I can go to hell"
是什么意思
一学生说："我下地狱，它们都很在乎"
另一学生（都是被点起来的）说：
"尽管它们都care，我还是能下地狱"
老师哈哈笑道：I'm sorry but it's all wrong
这句跟前面一样，也是反着来的
意思是说：
"我就是下地狱，它们（指星星）也不在乎"
反了、反了，老师喊道
跟着急停说：知道怎么把
"反了"二字
译成英语吗

202

返Pooh

讲到*Winnie-the-Pooh*时
老师问：知道"Pooh"是什么意思吗？
有学生说：是"噗噗"的意思

老师又问：Are you sure？
一学生说：就是
《小熊维尼》的意思

老师说：都不是
中文翻译更错
学生问：那你说是什么意思呢？

老师说："Pooh"，就是
我们每天都拉的那个
shit

全班的口，张得像"O"
随即"扑哧、扑哧"
地笑了，听起来颇像"Pooh"

老师放了一个视频，说：
看见没？苍蝇围着小熊鼻子转
以为那是一坨屎

等学生大笑完
老师说：这就是这本全球畅销书
的原始来历

老师跟着说：这也是中国
文化和英国文化
的重小区别

前者有shit说shit，绝不说不是shit
Pooh就是Pooh
不是Pooh就不是Pooh

后者却要keeping up appearances
老师停下问：这是啥意思？
一学生语塞，另一学生也语塞

老师说：就一个字：装！
不是装B，那太难听
而是装A

整个教室又笑成了洞开的"O"
老师继续说：中国的翻译太装A了
什么《小熊维尼》，完全是shit！

如果你们以后做翻译
我送你们四个字：
归真返Pooh！ [183]

该、不该

不该大写的大写了
像这样：YuanTouzhu

不该小写的小写了
像这样：haha, I want to say...

该说"I"时她说"we"
像这样："We should really cherish the life with our parents..."

[有人问了：Why do you all sound so didactic
'we', 'we', 'we', all the time?

---

183 16/4/17, HBL.

I don't understand. Are you a representative of all?
Can you speak for all? If not, why always 'we', 'we', and 'we'?]

该复数时她单数
像这样："For those who…inhale some fresh new air and pull yourself together"

该隔开时她偏不隔开
像这样："to make it better.Keeping passionate…"

该仔细时他偏不仔细
像这样："All the writes need your precious comments"

五十几人的学英语的研究生
居然没一个人看出！

该、不该
学English？

该、不该
teach英文？

That is the
Question[184]

钱

1.
Brunswick Street, Fitzroy
靠近No. 303, Marios Café
停车费照样贵：一小时4澳元

---

184 7/4/17, HBL.

掏出零钱一看
凑足也才两块多
钱包只有十五块

拿了五块换了零币
往表里塞钱：吞了两块
吐出两块，开了一张半小时票

2.
烦！半小时后回来
到一家Bar
拿10块钱换了5个2 dollars

一口气往表里塞了4个
硬的2元币
拉出一张2小时的单子

一看：哦，霾高！
前面一车贴了红色罚单
后面一车也贴了，红色罚单

3.
将近两小时后
跟出版社老总聊完回来
路遇一家Closing Down的书店

多么好的新书、多厚、多精美
每本降价到6元
买了三本：Gorky的 *My Childhood*（260页）

Patrick White的 *The Vivisector*（602页）
Vladimir Nabokov的 *The Origin of Laura*（278页）
总共价格：18块

4.
看看时间尚早
去了Preston的Cash Converters
提了一大袋东西：

儿子不要的电子闹钟（还是好的）
我没用过的胶卷和相纸（全新的）
苹果电脑的adapters和数码相机的接线（从未用过的）

瘦瘦的小伙子一看就说：
闹钟要，其他都不要
你看5 bucks如何？

又kindly告诉我：
你去街对面那家电脑店
看他们要不要

5.
我去了
出来一个脸黑黑的宽宽的人
说：你要多少钱？

我说：你说你出多少价吧
他说：我要是说出来，你会觉得
我的answer肯定terrible

他一说，我一听，觉得并不terrible：
每个苹果adapter五澳元
我拿了十块钱就走

6.
路上我想起，其中那个
是前两年在香港买的
花了我250个港币

207

7.
走到车边，我一看：糟
好像轮缘上有擦痕
车门外也有，还很新！

用手抹去擦掉的一小片皮
什么都没说
我就开车走了[185]

Shengqing bingmao

她写了一首shengqing
bingmao的诗

and the poet instantly
turned that into something like this:

She's written a poem
of sound and sensibilities, both ripe[186]

Tzu

'Tzu', 'Tzu', 他费劲地说
还是发得不像
听上去倒很像"纸"和"猪"的结合

不过，当他把笔下主人公定位成
Lang Tzu, 相信那就是中国人
的雅号时，他还是触摸到了某种

类似骨头的东西
他说：You always have 'Tzu'

---

185 6/3/17, Kingsbury.
186 23/3/17, HBL.

Kong Tzu, Lao Tzu, Chuang Tzu, don't ya?

So, here I am, with Lang Tzu（浪子）
我hahaha了一会儿
忽然觉得，他也有那么点Tzu味了

中国的五月长假无处可去
我在家看书，看到了闵子
说他："处人论事之法"

"天生的一段中平之气"[187]
于是那段往事
又在心中Tzu现出来[188]

鱼

再脏的水　　　也有鱼
太阳发亮的时候　　　鱼　　出　　群出

泥色的鱼　　青涩的鱼　　有色鱼种的鱼
在那么脏的水里长大　心脏　水脏　　　天脏

依然像鱼一样游动　肥的游起来照样　不显肥
也似乎 丝毫没有　　知道自己会被吃　之虞

脏水是其生命的保护　鱼怕人 一有人影出现 鱼
就　　鱼之天天　　龟也是 一头在岩石上 晒太阳

的龟　是最　　讨厌人的　　堡垒 入水　　　速度
比眼　　　快　比手　　疾 不比 笨舌 笨

---

187 引号中的两句引文，均引自[明]吕坤，《呻吟语》。上海大学出版社，2012
，132页。
188 29/4/17, HBL.

无痛鱼流的时代　　　雨　　也带上了鱼　意　　yu　　吁
长鱼短叹　　鱼的雨 在阳光的皮肤下

切入无 我对鱼　　　　的爱　　　　似乎无人　　可及
影子飘逸　　　漂移　　　　影追着影　　深深地 动

烂鱼头 还在游 一个国家的沉 沦　　　一些水的自　　来
一生不求发表的鱼　　一死也不　　比人伟小　　比鱼更鱼

这些　黑色的动作　这些　流转的动　　词　　这些　活
爱水及鱼爱鱼及影爱影及肉爱肉及深爱无及空爱善及恶爱日及夜　鱼洞

鱼　　只是　一种　　想　　法　　非法地游　　历　　充满毒汁
死鱼眼 发白泛白　　鱼肚黑 活到下 面去　比低更

低　　音的喉管　　从地底 天的地 云的泥 人的兽皮
三十三gan dong　　　五十五tiao　　yu　　七十八ge zi 呼儿嗨哟

笔名: 鱼裸　艺名: 被吃　字: 裸到只剩皮 出生地: 刺　籍贯: 无
用鱼做了鞋跟　用鱼装精液　　用鱼涂眼蓝　　用鱼生仔　　用鱼high

把鱼子流下来, 我是说, 留下来, 煮熟了吃
那是鱼的孩子呀, 是, 孩子才最好吃, 比如烤猪仔, 比如胎盘, 比如

我的头被劈成两半　　我的肉身　　　被凌迟 被煮熟
我何以知之　我是鱼 最受人欢迎的尸　　　　体

探　　讨鱼　四点睡水　　竖弯勾兑　　现　　3D鱼在打印
需4至　5小时 你说得对　　耗资约　　四五千元

旦　　夕鱼 阳西 上鱼　　推时已入下　水道　路路无为
什么　　　老幺鱼 有一横才成　　　王　　即亡

农家乐英语　　　　　黑描　白绘鱼乌托邦派　　出所　鱼
过去时的鱼将来时了　　虚拟鱼气　　在地鱼里游的狱

210

欧阳鱼的昱　　乌鸦鱼 浮云鱼 即景鱼 刀落鱼 风过鱼
windfall鱼　　　weepie鱼　　　broad smile鱼　　　　quick smile鱼

Prynne鱼　　　内部资料鱼　　妊娠纹fish　　镜子fish fish鱼 健身fish
静　　电鱼　悼悼鱼欲　　望鱼 子　　丰满　　　　族

Ich danke innen 鱼上就把你忘记了　　快鱼加鞭　　长莫　 衷一　 穷
二是爱 这条好大　　而无　　裆　　　　鱼肉人 参　　　　　　加

法酷　儿　　子息同时放　 两个　逼迫于 计有　生之　月
自杀算 了　　无声　　　李好像 到美　　去了　日得

道多　鱼死网 泼妇　好多水 溅摄像 头道血 好生了
打得打得打　不　　得　　青鱼蛙 打桩鱼机　记鱼事本

无休无止的fish鱼　　离fish婚　　微鱼博 大精　神经分
我爱你鱼　　积鱼木　　　继鱼续 狗尾巴鱼草　文章鱼

鱼肛门　　白带鱼　　鱼里鱼气　鱼肚黑红　色迷
水牢中的鱼　不必　谷歌　不必youtube　照样毒在其中 依然ha

ppy　鱼生错了　　不如诗 而像寺 流氓鱼 婚鱼
净身高185以上的鱼　这鱼牙齿好难看　　高跟鞋鱼　插入鱼

总是素颜地在游　　小家碧鱼　　鱼丸子 鱼秃子 鱼小三
鱼老四 鱼丑人 鱼诗人 清水之地　　不食鱼

Voices

One said it's a tewu guojia, a Nation of Secret Agents
One said wo xiang ni, I think you
One said it's fulan touding, rotten through
One said wo fachu, I grew timid
One said chizao yao wandan de, it's going to be finished sooner or later
One said wo zui taoyan bianpao, I most heartily detest firecrackers
One said wo haishi xiang ni, I still think you
One said da chengshi you shenme hao, what's good about big cities
One said that's jew in you
One said labuchu jiushi labuchu, if you can't pull you can't pull
One said shi er houyi, poetry till you end
One said but you are kidding
One said niandu shiren buxing, poets of the year no good
One said bu fazhan yeshi ying daoli, non-development also a hard reason
One said shui huaile, xin jiu huaile, bad water, bad heart
One said wo xiang ni, I think you
One said wusuowei, past caring
One said fuzhou, city of comforting
One said linghun zai jiao, soul calling
One said yiqie guiyu wu, everything gone to nothing[189]

Miss Takes

Is a girl that I thoughts I love
Her first name: Error
Which translates into Chinese as "爱娜"
Her last name: Takes
Which, in Chinese, is "她伊克斯"
And it changes from time to time
When she take me

---

189 9/5/13, YSH.

She call herself: Miss Took（涂客小姐）
And proudly claim
That she is Miss Taken（她肯小姐）
I like the way she look and took
As she often say she do and knews
Despite my refusal
On many an occasion
That I am not her mann
When she declare poetry poultry
I have to agree
That she really deserve
The name: Miss Taken Took

8.32am

这个人，如果你让他当国家主席
他肯定要下令：
所有人都跟我起来：读诗

这个人，如果你让他当某国总统
他肯定要order：
check the new things out, without any delay

这个人，只能当他自己的一国主席和总统
于是他order自己：早上第一时间写诗
死后让别人读去

Place names Hong Kong, a random sonnet list

Chinese	English	Pinyin	Meaning
九龙	Kowloon	jiulong	Nine Dragons
长沙湾村	Cheung Sha Wan Estate	changsha wan cun	Long Sand Bay Village
黄竹坑	Wong Chuk Hang	huang zhu keng	Yellow Bamboo Pit
打磚街	Ta Chuen Street	da zhuan jie	Beat Brick Street
铜锣湾	Causeway Bay	tong luo wan	Copper Gong Bay
尖沙咀	Tsim Sha Tsui	jian sha zui	Sharp Sand Mouth
英皇道	King's Road	ying huang dao	English Emperor Road
油塘	Yau Tong	you tang	Oil Pond
健康街	Kin Hong Street	jiankang jie	Healthy Street
沙田火炭山尾街	Shan Mei Street, Fo Tan, Sha Tin	shatian, huotan, shanwei jie	Mountain Tail Street, Fiery Charcoal, Sandy Field
横龙街	Wang Lung Street	heng long jie	Cross Dragon Street
环凤街	Wan Fung Street	huan feng jie	Encircling Phoenix Street
西洋菜街	Sai Yeung Choy Street	xi yang cai jie	Western Foreign Vegetables Street

吖九孨

啊，王噶，啊，王嘎，啊，王孨，王孨，王孨
啊王孨，啊王孨，王孨王孨王孨
啊亡孨，啊亡孨，啊亡孨
啊汪王网望孨孨孨
啊王孨，啊王孨，啊王孨，啊王孨，啊王孨，啊王孨，啊王孨，啊

王尕，
啊王尕尕，啊王尕尕尕，啊王尕尕尕尕
啊翘尕，啊九尕，啊九尕，啊九尕，啊九尕尕尕
啊九尕尕尕尕啊九尕尕尕尕啊九尕尕尕尕啊九尕尕尕尕
啊九尕尕尕尕啊九尕尕尕尕啊九尕尕尕尕啊九尕尕尕尕
啊九尕尕尕尕啊九尕尕尕尕啊九尕尕尕尕啊九尕尕尕尕
啊九尕尕尕尕啊九尕尕尕尕啊九尕尕尕尕啊九尕尕尕尕
啊九尕尕尕尕啊九尕尕尕尕啊九尕尕尕尕啊九尕尕尕尕
啊九尕尕尕尕啊九尕尕尕尕啊九尕尕尕尕啊九尕尕尕尕
啊九尕尕尕尕啊九尕尕尕尕啊九尕尕尕尕啊九尕尕尕尕
啊九尕尕尕尕啊九尕尕尕尕啊九尕尕尕尕啊九尕尕尕尕
啊九尕尕尕尕啊九尕尕尕尕啊九尕尕尕尕啊九尕尕尕尕
啊九尕尕尕尕啊九尕尕尕尕啊九尕尕尕尕啊九尕尕尕尕
啊九尕尕尕尕啊九尕尕尕尕啊九尕尕尕尕啊九尕尕尕尕
啊，王噶，啊，王嘎，啊，王尕，王尕，王尕
啊王尕，啊王尕，王尕王尕王尕
啊亡尕，啊亡尕，啊亡尕
啊汪王网望尕尕尕
啊王尕，啊王尕，啊王尕，啊王尕，啊王尕，啊王尕，啊王尕，啊王尕，
啊王尕尕，啊王尕尕尕，啊王尕尕尕尕
啊翘尕，啊九尕，啊九尕，啊九尕，啊九尕尕尕

回忆

☞
那波兰女人一听我说是从中国来的
就说：
Oh, I adore China
☞
那法国男人一听我提到 Michel Houellebecq
就说：
Oh, I hate him

☞
我没话找话，又说：

看过戴思杰的《巴尔扎克和小裁缝》了吗？

他说：这书名一听就不想看，因为我讨厌Balzac

☞
22岁的哈萨克姑娘玛蒂娜对我说：

I want to go to Italy because I love it so much

我说：千万别去

☞
法国男人对阿尔达克说：

I like your tie

我一翻译，他就把领带解下来，说：给你

☞
芬兰诗人说：我们那儿搞文学活动

是不唱颂歌的。Intellectuals criticize, you know

我说：It's the same in Australia

☞
那个叫瑟利克的诗人每次见到我都说：

万岁，万万岁

我说：应该说：万岁、万岁、万万岁！

☞
那个吉尔吉斯坦的诗人总是坚持要跟我"干杯"

随后便把喝干的酒杯倒立在头顶上面

表示一滴不剩

☞
伏特加喝下去的感觉

仿佛喉咙腾起了一把火

肚子里却是空的

☞
他们每到一处都要拉尿

喝伏特加，用砍下来的塑料水瓶底

从塑料袋里抓肉吃

☞
那个二十多年不写诗的作协秘书
每次见面都要用英语盛赞
毛泽东的伟大，听不进我的反对

☞
朋友告诉我：无树大平原一到冬天
到处都是狼。有时带枪也打不完
直到狼群扑上，连人带马把你吃光

☞
还告诉我：30公里的赛马
胜者总是7岁的小男或小女
奖品是三部崭新越野车

☞
那是因为他们身轻如叶
让马在无负重的状态下飞奔
远胜过年轻的职业赛手

☞
朋友还说：儿子要我明年给他买一匹马
我们这儿最作兴的就是骑马了
养一匹马，把儿子骑大

☞
而且我们爱喝马奶
最新鲜的马奶
我一气可喝三四十碗

☞
我喝不下去
只觉得很酸
还是勉强，喝了一杯

☞
每天吃的都是"别什巴尔马克"（抓肉）
马肉，以及马肉，以及马肉
我想起了《水浒》：大块肉切来！

☞
第一次骑马的感觉:
踩着马镫的脚, 好像踏着半空的叶片
踏浪也比这踏实

☞
我在记者招待会上说:
When I come back again
I shall learn how to ride a horse

☞
我问俄罗斯诗人: 普金怎样了?
他不回答, 却问:
Do you speak German?

☞
亚美尼亚诗人总是看着我
点头、微笑、举杯
我却无法用他的语言问他, 有关大屠杀的事

☞
我看见那个俄罗斯翻译舒展手臂, 放在椅背
俄罗斯女诗人的椅背上
这使我想起从前, 一个中国男诗人, 也是这样把手, 放在两个女诗人的椅背上

☞
无法用语言交流, 其实并不痛苦
他们一个劲地讲, 我一个劲地吃
就像在澳洲, 那些出席华人酒宴的白人

☞
哦, 对了, 这些诗人朗诵, 从来不用稿子
他们把诗写好, 背诵下来
又让我想起, 那个来自新西兰的华人诗人大律师Chan

☞
我们去国家图书馆的路上问路
那人停下来, 先问好, 再一一握手
然后指路

☞
一块人民币值多少坚戈？
我来查查看：
54.92

☞
是的，都说那儿女少男多
适合中国男士
但人家已经示威了，反对哈族姑娘外嫁

☞
一个不认识的人对我大喊大叫
朋友接腔，叫他文明点
后来才说：他见你是中国人才——

☞
见到一个副县长
二女儿在布里斯班读书
大女儿已从赫尔辛基毕业

☞
但中饭没来陪局
因为昨天正县长车祸与妻身亡
要去参加葬礼

☞
回来后才想起
该写这一句的：
我用云，洗了面

(Kazakhstan, late 2018)

义乌一行

-黑人的眼，长在义乌的唇上，哦，不，我是说在早餐厅

-窗外传来打喷嚏声，控诉一样响，让我笑了，说了一句：这狗日的！

-问那人：哪里来？他说：Uganda，然后问你呢，我说：Of course China

219

-又是电梯，昨晚，弄清对面是Iran后，他说：We challenge America

-好大的乳，从侧面看，黑的，黑衣服，of那张，坐在角落的黑女

-调色板上：垃圾的浓郁美，眼睛从屁眼长到腋窝的脚下去了

-那黑人说：I am a poet，我一惊，一扭头，看见了义乌，乌干达的乌

-一切都是前定

-一整夜，就盯着那个女的，用白布，擦酒杯的里面，擦外面，反转着放下来

-我用酒杯喝水，到后来，觉得喝的都是酒

-能不能不喜欢我的东西？这样，就不能做成商品了

-我跟他确认了，果然是shisha，啊，吸霞。他说：only this one

-快去给我找个乌溜溜的黑妞来吧，我是说义乌溜溜的

-史书说：顺毛乌鬼国、卷毛乌鬼国。现在是：顺毛卷毛义乌gui国

-伸头一看：印度人。再伸头一看：阿拉伯人。再伸头一看：哟，黄种外国人

-牙签？有！在下面餐厅，我看见一个黑人，在剔牙，剔白牙

-夜里，我不喝酒不吃肉，只想要个女人，来给我吸个霞

-蓝天白云：有蓝天，无白云，只剩每年千万和盼亿，以及看不见的乌江

-我是说义乌江

-一个很阿拉伯的人，站在一大堆货物旁，什么都不像

-女人的脸，在灯光下，特别发亮

220

-黑人看回来，不做声，我想象，我就是他，也看回去

-一夜无话，我无聊，我看她，也无撩，坐在前台，看手机

-做商人的诗人，没从商里看出诗机，却从诗里，看出商机

-"此处违章事故较多。你已进入嘉兴海宁市"

-"当前车速一百零二。前方三百米有监控拍照"

-黑人把义，变得更乌

-诗人一来，就把画室的调色板搞大

-我：走向荒芜，渐渐远离。你：上上下下，舒舒服服

-整个义乌，放不下一本书。画室里没有，诗人店里，只有货的样品

-一大早，一个黑人，抱着一抱书，在我面前拐个弯，走了

-"盖浇饭、盖浇饭"，声音穿过商店的高铁走廊传过来，我看见背影了

-人很好，床太大，夜太长，男人对柜台后面的女人说

-歌中唱道：像假话一样绚烂

-活到六十还不自杀，那就太商人了，还在等下一个零

- '"每颗雨滴都是单独的"，虽然小，但因为单独而有力量，胜过乌合之众'

-"义乌合之众"，我随手在纸上写道

-我就给你起个名字吧。叫什么呢？爱乌及义乌

(June 2018, in Yiwu, Zhejiang, China)

Acknowledgements

The phrase "flag of permanent defeat" is taken from Ernest Hemingway's *The Old Man and The Sea.*

'Soul Diary: Key-words', *Triptych Poets*, Canberra: Blemish Books, 2011.

'Soul diary', an excerpt, *LiNQ*, Vol., 31, No. 1, 2004, pp. 72-3.

'Soul Diary: Key-words', *Southerly* (Sydney), Vol., 62, No., 1, 2002, pp. 104-105.

'Place names Hong Kong, a random sonnet list', *Southerly*, Vol., 70, No. 2, 2010, p. 124.

'Voices', *Australian Poetry Journal*, Issue 1, Vol. 5, 2015, p. 26.

The poem, '山重水复' (written in English with a Chinese title), translated into Estonian by Doris Kareva, published in *SIRP*, 2/9/11, p. 26.